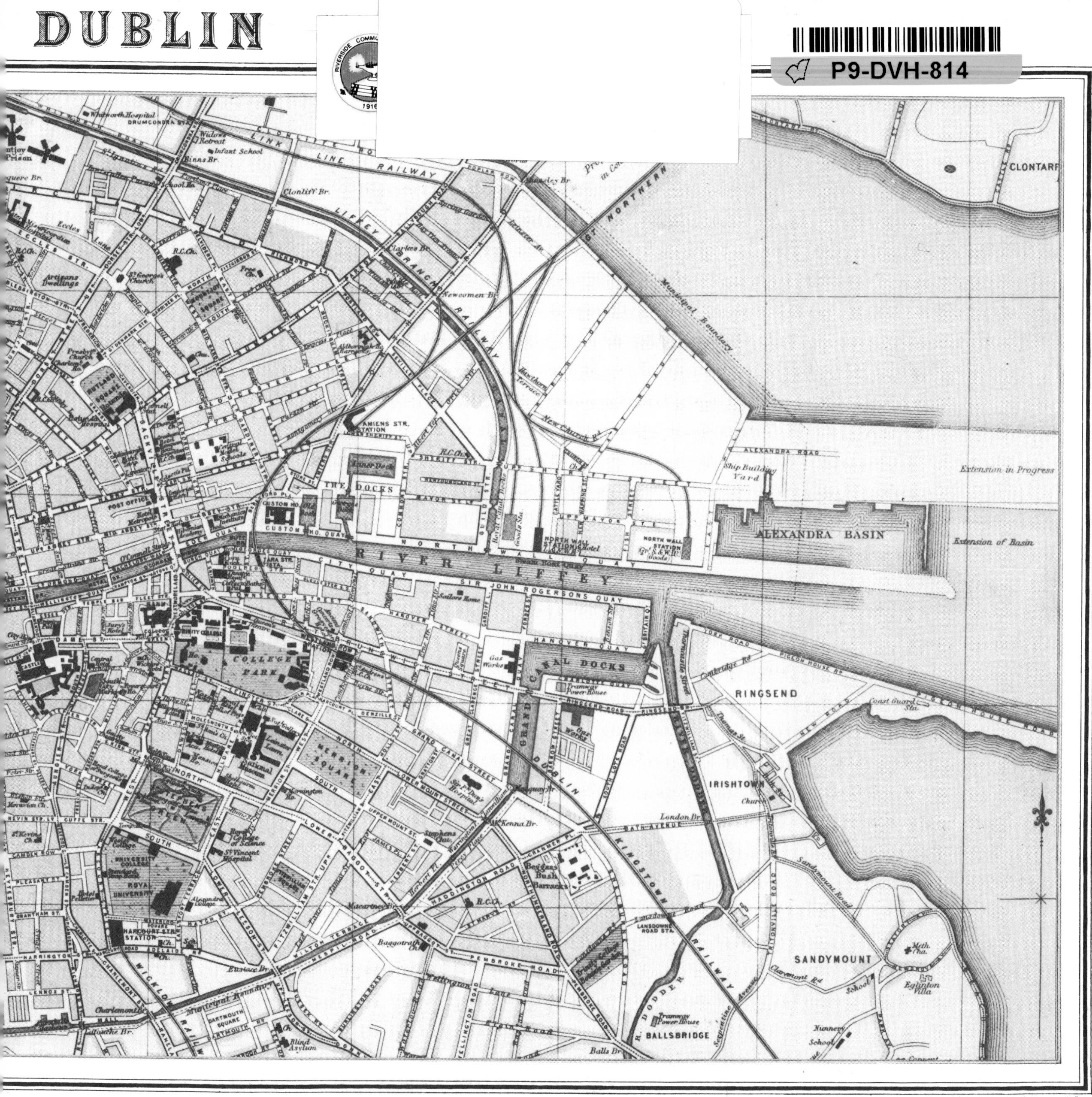

DUBLIN
CLONTARF
Whitworth Hospital
Drumcondra Sta.
Widows Retreat
Infant School
Binns Br.
Link Line Railway
Clonliff Br.
Liffey Branch Railway
Gt. Northern
Municipal Boundary
Clarkes Br.
Newcomen Br.
Eccles St.
Artizans Dwellings
St. George's Church
Mountjoy Square
Rutland Square
Rotunda Hospital
Amiens Str. Station
The Docks
Inner Dock
Custom Ho.
Custom Ho. Quay
Post Office
O'Connell Street
North Wall Station
North Wall Quay
River Liffey
City Quay
Sir John Rogersons Quay
Alexandra Road
Ship Building Yard
Extension in Progress
Alexandra Basin
Extension of Basin
New Church Rd.
Hawthorn Terrace
Trinity College
College Park
Hanover Quay
Grand Canal Docks
Gas Works
Ringsend
Ringsend Road
York Road
Pigeon House Rd.
Coast Guard Sta.
Irishtown
London Br.
Bath Avenue
Merrion Square
St. Stephens Green
Grand Canal Street
Lower Mount Street
McKenna Br.
Beggars Bush Barracks
Haddington Road
Royal University
University College
Harcourt Str. Station
Macartney Br.
Baggotrath Ch.
Pembroke Road
Lansdowne Road Sta.
Kingstown Railway
Wicklow Railway
Municipal Boundary
Sandymount
Sandymount Road
Eglinton Villa
R. Dodder
Tramway Power House
Ballsbridge
Balls Br.
Blind Asylum
Dartmouth Square
Charlemont Br.
Leeson St.
Kevin Str.
Camden Row
Harrington St.
Eustace Br.
Wellington Road
Serpentine Avenue

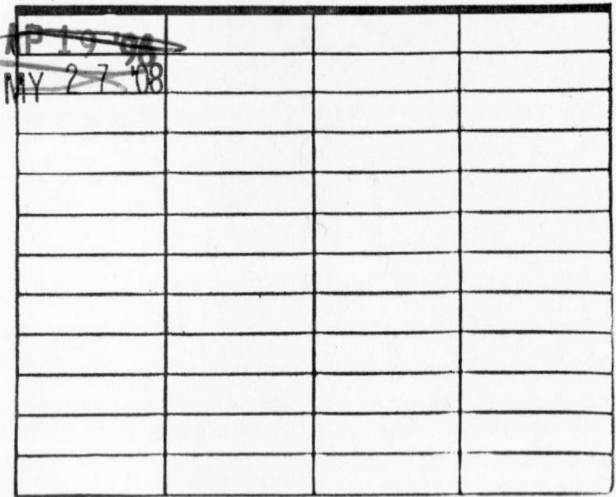

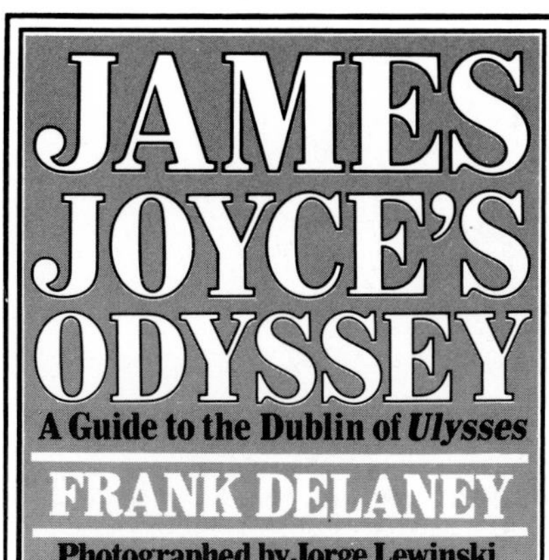

JAMES JOYCE'S ODYSSEY

A Guide to the Dublin of *Ulysses*

FRANK DELANEY

Photographed by Jorge Lewinski

JAMES JOYCE'S ODYSSEY

A Guide to the Dublin of *Ulysses*

FRANK DELANEY

Photographed by Jorge Lewinski

Holt, Rinehart and Winston New York

First published in the United States in 1982 by Holt, Rinehart and Winston, 383 Madison Avenue, New York, New York 10017.

Library of Congress Cataloging in Publication Data
1. Joyce, James, 1882-1941 – Ulysses
2. Dublin (Dublin) in literature.
3. Dublin (Dublin)—Description—Guide-books.
4. Joyce, James, 1882–1941—Homes and haunts—Ireland—Dublin.
5. Authors, Irish—20th century—Biography.
I. Lewinski, Jorge. II. Title.
PR6019.09U638 1982 823'.912 81–83276
ISBN 0–03–060457–5 AACR2

ISBN: 0-03-060457-5

First American Edition

Book design: Sharyn Troughton

Printed in Great Britain
10 9 8 7 6 5 4 3 2 1

This book is dedicated to my three sons,
Frank, Bryan and Owen Delaney,
who are already Dubliners and who
may yet become Joyceans.

EST LEATHER
ONLY USED
IRISH SEWING Ltd.
17
18
SINGER

CONTENTS

The distant Seychelles are not so remote
Nor Ctesiphon as ultimately dead
As this damp square round which tired echoes float
Of something brilliant that George Moore once said:
Where, still, in pitch-pine snugs pale poets quote
Verses rejected by the Bodley Head
For in this drained aquarium no breeze
Deposits pollen from more fertile shores
Or kills the smell of long unopened drawers
That clings forever to these dripping trees.
Where Bloom once wandered, gross and ill-at-ease,
Twice-pensioned heroes of forgotten wars
With misplaced confidence demand applause
Shouting stale slogans on the Liffey quays.

Osbert Lancaster, *Afternoons with Baedeker*

INTRODUCTION

Reading *Ulysses* is one of the pleasures of life. It is a vast, entertaining, funny, absorbing, exciting, complex, immensely *enjoyable* novel, a book to get lost in, a book to take to a desert island, a book to keep by your bedside and discover each day something new, a book to be quoted from, recalled, discussed, contemplated, bequeathed, bestowed, above all to be relished, savoured, a work of intelligence and delight. But ever since it was published on James Joyce's fortieth birthday, the 2nd of February, 1922, generations of readers have faltered. "I *will* finish it this time!" muttered the cinemagoers when Joseph Strick's film of *Ulysses* was shown: Joyce's novel is still, to many, a literary obstacle course and the reader whose stamina fails often feels guilty.

But is this surprising? The sheer length of the text (over three hundred thousand words), Joyce's genius with language (a rock-garden of classical references), the many interconnecting levels on which the author built his work (topographical, musical, theological, physiological, political, mythical) and the range of writing techniques (streams of consciousness, internal monologues, buried fact, synecdoche) all dumbfound the non-academic reader and exercise the scholar.

Ulysses has always controlled its readers, even the most learned, sending devoted students off to dig into every relevant archive (often inventing new ones in the process) and, alas, daunting those who just want to enjoy James Joyce. What other twentieth-century author has spawned such a huge body of academic and esoteric research? Universities, especially in America, dedicate entire areas of their English departments to him; translations, however unlikely given the particularity of the text, abound – Korean, Japanese, as well as European languages; Joyce's life and literature have consumed careers, imaginations, bibliographies. And though this body of academic attention would have delighted the author himself who desired to "keep the professors busy for years", has it not, by its size and daunting diligence, come between Joyce and the non-academic reader, the enthusiast?

Certainly even the most animated conversation about *Ulysses* will frequently include the comment: "I never managed it fully, tried several times, but somehow I couldn't get it finished". A pity – the perseverance is so well worth it, if only for the fun and the jokes, and the marvellous writing ability of the man, the superb use of language, the parody, the satire, the understanding of human nature.

A pity too, that *Ulysses* should somehow have been lodged outside the reach of the people about whom it was written. Joyce saw himself as essentially the chronicler of the common man. His companions were the "hundred-headed rabble of the cathedral close", waiters and tailors and fruit-sellers and porters: "nobody in any of my books is worth more than a hundred pounds". And he believed that the key to human nature lay in observing the commonest acts of man, ordering a drink, eating a meal, opening an umbrella, folding a newspaper. *Ulysses* and its behaviour exhibits Joyce's beliefs to the full. It was his third book of four – *Dubliners,* a collection of short stories; *A*

Portrait of the Artist as a Young Man, an autobiographical novel; and, after *Ulysses, Finnegans Wake,* "The Wake", as its affectionately called, which especially gave Joyce a reputation for obscurity, for recycling the English language.

"I want," said Joyce to a friend in Zurich, "to give a picture of Dublin so complete that if the city one day suddenly disappeared from the earth it could be reconstructed out of my book." He had been born and educated in Dublin, lived, loved, borrowed and begged in Dublin, was enhanced, betrayed and finally excluded by Dublin and up to the time he died, thirty-seven years after his self-imposed exile, chosen ascetically, exercised artistically, he taxed native Dubliners who visited him with his ability to remember the names and numbers of the shops and the houses in correct sequence.

Ulysses is James Joyce's incantation to, for and of Dublin. It was designed by him as a detailed account of ordinary life on an ordinary Dublin day, and he planned each movement of each character on each street as though he were playing chess. He placed them in houses he knew, drinking in pubs he had frequented, walking on cobblestones he retraced. He made the very air of Dublin, the atmosphere, the feeling, the place, almost indistinguishable, certainly inseparable, from his human characters – Dublin *is* a character in *Ulysses,* the "womancity" with her skirts lifted. Consequently, a feeling for Dublin as Joyce portrayed it, a knowledge of the city as it might have been in his time, and a modern catalogue of the geography of *Ulysses* may help to loosen the novel's bindings. A journey through its pages is a glistening, aromatic, atmospheric voyage in the company of believable, likeable, culpable human beings with ordinary vices, virtues and traits - recognisable people, comic, tragic, vulnerable, uncertain, carnal, aggressive, defensive, passionate, aloof, romantic, cynical.

At its simplest – dare I use the word! – *Ulysses* is a story of some random ramblings through a large part of Dublin on a single day, Thursday, 16th of June, 1904. Paths cross and criss-cross, characters pass by each other, knowingly and unknowingly. They greet, ignore, applaud and insult each other – their lives and the life of the city intermingle naturally and normally in the teeming streets. They are not remarkable people in any late-twentieth-century media-gilded way; few of these citizens would ever make the newspaper columns except by the announcement of a birth, marriage or death. But they are credible in their ordinariness, comic and tragic in their predicament and monumentally luminous, illuminating in their humanity. In the personalities of Leopold Bloom and his heaving wife Molly, Stephen Dedalus (Joyce himself at the age of twenty-two, the age he left Dublin) and various other assorted characters, Joyce drew, as he set out to, a map of human nature, a map whose symbols are everyday incidents, joys, tragedies, encounters, disappointments, boastings, betrayals, laughter and pain – a suitable case for the widest range of academic, philosophical and literary investigation.

I who dishevelled ways forsook
To hold the poets' grammar-book,
Bringing to tavern and to brothel
The mind of witty Aristotle,
Lest bards in the attempt should err
Must here be my interpreter:
Wherefore receive now from my lip
Peripatetic scholarship.

Taken out of context, the opening lines of Joyce's ballad *The Holy Office,* though intended differently (a vicious satire on old Dublin enemies) can be searched for a hint, no more, of the motivation for *Ulysses.* And then, as always, the danger with

Joyce is that just as you interpret him – or think you do – some other aspect, some digression, some pun, reference or vagary diverts you and once again he is the computer you cannot beat. He is, finally, his own interpreter. So why write a book of part-criticism, part-interpretation, part-illumination, a guide, any guide, to *Ulysses*? The answer is, simply, enthusiasm. (And, like Everest, it was *there* – the two efforts, scaling his heights, skirting precipice and crevasse, are not dissimilar!) I know I cannot possibly explicate, or even exhibit, every single reference on every single page – I only hope that the occasional delights I touch or trigger contribute to the overall score on the pinball machine. I know too, that a work of guidance to, or interpretation of, *Ulysses* which will be total and comprehensive in itself is perhaps impossible, certainly out of reach to someone not yet turned forty – and who has the ordinary necessities of life, such as eating and sleeping to attend to!

I am aware of, and am consumed with respect for, the huge body of academic work which Joyce has inspired. For example, who could possibly emulate, improve upon, the impeccable Richard Ellmann biography, the standard bible for all Joyce students? Agreed that there remains other work to be done; Anthony Burgess who, in his own novels, responds so warmly to Joyce, believes that the sequel to *Ulysses* must be written. But this book does not belong in any of those areas – this is a work of happy, gazetteering enthusiasm, sparked by a desire to share in the delights of an author whose city surrounded me for years, tinged me for ever. This is a plain man's guide to a novel, perhaps *the* novel, of the plain man. As befits such a project, the text of *Ulysses* from which I have quoted (trying wherever possible not to break the quotation internally – his prose is as music) is the 1969 edition published in the United Kingdom by Penguin, in paperback. In some cases where he did not, I have used capital letters in the interests of plainness, as I have decided, too, not to use the method of indicating speech – *Ulysses* employed the dash "–".

There is another notion underlying this book. *Ulysses* may, if you wish, become a guidebook, a literary Baedeker, by which a trip to Dublin becomes enlivened. Indeed, much of the more distinguished academic work, such as Clive Hart's, has examined that aspect. And after all, Joyce designed the novel from his own knowledge of the city, from details supplied by friends, relatives, books, newspapers – and from the information contained in *Thom's Directory of the United Kingdom of Great Britain and Ireland – Dublin Edition, 1904*. Each year this tome gazetted, alongside government and commerce, the city of Dublin, street by house, house by occupant and Joyce, for the purposes of *Ulysses*, interrogated Thom's. The characters and their bits and pieces were in his head already – he used *Thom's* to find them rooms to live in, places to go.

Dublin escaped the Second World War and the city of *Ulysses* is still there, forlorn, dishevelled and available. But only just available. Many of Joyce's streets have keeled over quietly, lanes have been suffocated, houses are lying, wounded and dying, on the kerbside. Only the big streets have survived and not always as Joyce utilised them. Even Mr. Bloom's house, Number Seven, Eccles Street, the most famous address in English literature, is on the verge of disappearing under the developer's pencil. Other areas have changed utterly. In fifty years from now it may well be that, public buildings and principal streets apart, the Dublin of *Ulysses* will be no more.

Yet Joyce's mist clings. It is to be found in the dingy lanes off the quays, in the web of streets leading to the river, through the railings at "Trinity's surly front", in Grafton Street still "gay with housed awnings", in the National Library, at the Martello Tower, preserved with dignity at Sandycove, behind the cypresses in the cemetery at

Glasnevin. Like old glass jars, parts of the city have bottled Joyce's smoky vapours.

Which is only as it should be. For long enough Joyce was reviled in his native city: Ireland in the 'Twenties was hardly sufficiently liberal to embrace an author who described woman as "an animal that micturates once a day, defecates once a week, menstruates once a month and parturates once a year": who satirised the principal ritual of the Roman Catholic Church (into which he was born) in his opening paragraph, and who described his native land as "the sow that eats her own farrow"! Nonetheless, as the years brought down benevolence, Joyce's genius was recognised and the city has come to regard its genius with that ironic affection it uses for compliments.

But if you have never read *Ulysses,* never visited Dublin, never known the work of James Joyce why do you need a guide to his odyssey? Well, he intended his work to be international, universal, the complete gazetteer of the human condition, a map of the body and the mind, as well as of the Dublin he knew. Leopold Bloom, Joyce's Common Man, leaves his home at eight o'clock on a Thursday morning in June, 1904, to buy his breakfast and returns finally, and sleeps at approximately two o'clock the following morning. In the hours between, he lands on the shores of many streets, endures misadventure and delight, tastes gall and honey before, as Homer's hero did, he regains the sanctuary of his terraced Ithaca where his wife spins at her loom of dreams. His voyage has taken him through the streets broad and narrow of Dublin on a parallel to one of the greatest adventure tales ever described – for the Isles of Greece read the streets of Dublin. If you accept, as a definition of the novel, the reflection of the human condition, Joyce's novel is the ultimate such exercise.

Who was this wayward genius, this odd, acerbic soul, who has been credited with changing the structure and course of the novel? He was a half-blind, irascible, impecunious spendthrift who quarrelled with his closest friends, made enemies of mere acquaintances, was a scathing critic, a devastating satirist, a man of immense imagination, learning and sheer brain-power. He lived most of his life in four cities, Dublin, Trieste, Zurich and Paris, and he was fifty-nine and famous when he died in 1941. Beckett took notes for him, Hemingway wrote letters to him, Proust asked him if he liked truffles.

Wrote one critic: "He wrote nothing that wasn't a masterpiece." Wrote another: "Mr. Joyce is a queasy undergraduate scratching his pimples." He opened Dublin's first cinema, the Volta in Mary Street, after he had persuaded some Italian businessmen to put up the money, and the rapt patrons sat for hours watching sepia waves washing a beach. Other failed ventures included the importation of Irish tweed into Italy, accounting for a bank in Rome, and litigation over real and/or imagined insults.

He was a delighted, devoted son, committed family man, remained in love with just one woman, whom he married after twenty-seven years of cohabitation. He was regarded by some literary critics and contemporaries – himself included – as the greatest writer since Shakespeare. Much of Joyce's work lay beneath its own surface. For example – at no point in *Ulysses* does he describe physically the streets of Dublin, yet you can recognise them. But in the National Library – by a pleasing coincidence the scene of an entire chapter in the novel – lies the famous Lawrence Collection, a wonderful, huge storehouse of photographs taken and preserved on glass plates by Robert French, a photographer, who worked for William Lawrence of O'Connell Street. The Lawrence Collection froze for ever Dublin as Joyce knew it and even though all the photographs reproduced in this book may not necessarily belong to the year 1904 (Lawrence's chronological cataloguing left something to be desired) they are of the Joycean period, that calm, pre-revolutionary period of Queen Victoria and her son, later King Edward VII. Robert French's photography all over Ireland embraced the period between 1880 and 1910 and the National Library acquired the forty thousand plates in 1942 for three hundred pounds.

When Jorge Lewinski, specially commissioned and committed, visited the scenes of *Ulysses,* he photographed them as much in a spirit of atmospheric enquiry as of geographical record. If on occasion you find it difficult to tell which pictures are Robert French's and which are Jorge Lewinski's – then, perhaps that, too, is a comment on Joyce.

So, with visual support, what of James Joyce's claim? Could Dublin, if required, be reconstructed out of the pages of *Ulysses*?

Well, should Joyce's comment be taken at face value? Always a dangerous thing to do with a man who after all, writing autobiographically, gave himself the name Dedalus, the mythological figure who devised the Labyrinth. To be regarded as an enigma was one of Joyce's better-known desires and therefore, whether Dublin could be rebuilt using *Ulysses* as a site-map is not, perhaps, the whole question, because did the architect mean physical or imaginative reconstruction? Or the means of finding out, the journey through Dublin and *Ulysses,* the hopeful travelling rather than the arrival, is that what Joyce intended? Maybe he wanted it to be a personal odyssey for each reader, an examination of self, enthusiasm? In which case. . .

FRANK DELANEY
London, 1981

TELEMACHUS

This Martello Tower, its original defensive menace muted, sits on a knuckle of Dublin coastline gnawed by the Irish Sea. Other such pocket-fortresses along the coast fell into decay, some were rescued as fashionably eccentric habitations and this one became a museum.

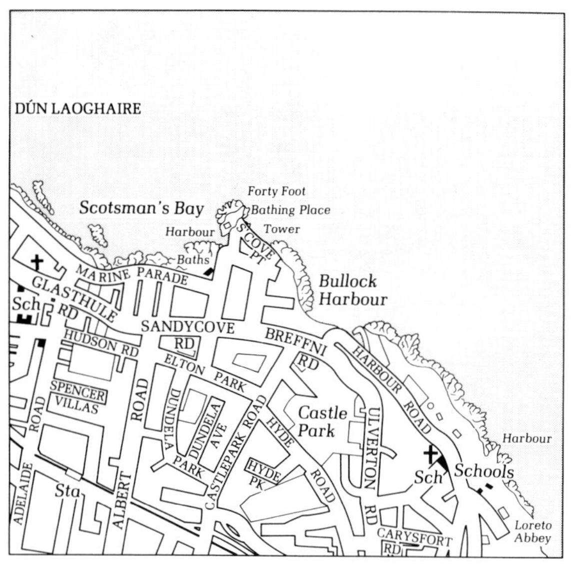

Leave Dublin, travel due south through Dun Laoire towards Dalkey and beyond the cluster of Glasthule village turn left into Sandycove Avenue West. Down the slope, adjacent to the Forty-Foot Bathing Place, you will find the Martello Tower and seasonally you may buy a ticket of admission, which reads:

> The Martello Tower at Sandycove, better known as James Joyce's Tower, was built in 1804 by the British in a series of defence measures to withstand a threatened Napoleonic invasion. The Tower, which is forty feet high with walls eight feet thick, was lived in by James Joyce in 1904 and provided the setting for part of the first chapter of *Ulysses*. It is now owned by the Eastern Regional Tourism Organisation who maintain it as a Joycean Museum.

On a Thursday night in 1904 three men lay asleep in the cold domed room of this tower. One, Samuel Chenevix Trench, had a nightmare about a black panther. He took his handgun, fired suddenly but harmlessly at the imaginary animal and went back to sleep. Not long afterwards he yelled again – same panther, different nightmare. Oliver St. John Gogarty, a wild medical student, grabbed the gun and fired gleefully at the pots and pans above the sleeping bed of the third man. This was James Joyce, who rose in fright, dressed in dudgeon and left to walk to Dublin in the rain.

The incident triggered Joyce's exile and planted the opening chapter of *Ulysses*. These three men are the characters whose conversation in and around the Martello Tower at Sandycove forms the opening episode. Samuel Chenevix Trench (who later blew his brains out, perhaps with the same revolver) appears as Haines the Englishman. Oliver St. John Gogarty, who fired at the pots and pans, is Buck Mulligan, mocker and roisterer. Most important is the author's depiction of himself, Stephen Dedalus as James Joyce.

Joyce had come to Sandycove by invitation, only six nights earlier, in September 1904, but had moodily outstayed the ebullient Gogarty's welcome. The coldness of Joyce's departure never thawed, even though Gogarty made several attempts at reconciliation, principally because he guessed, anxiously and correctly, that Joyce would lampoon him in literature. "He fears the lancet of my art as I fear that of his," is the cool observation which Joyce/Dedalus makes internally while being pilloried in the Tower by the irreverent medical student, Gogarty/Mulligan. And in time, indeed, Joyce exacted a humiliating literary revenge for Gogarty's nocturnal ballistics.

But why a Martello Tower? Apart from Joyce's interrupted repose there – Gogarty became a tenant in order to make it the Irish equivalent of the earth's navel-stone at Delphi, with himself as the Oracle – was it the imagery that appealed to Joyce, the round, smooth, impregnable, prominent fortification, a metaphor for his own personality? Or was it the fact that a Martello Tower seems a truncated version, a reducation, in phallic terms, of that other great Irish fortification, the Round Tower, used by monks to protect their sacred vessels and illuminated manuscripts from marauders?

In the days when Joyce stayed there Sandycove was already an orderly outpost of Dublin, a distant gardened suburb to which the middle classes had begun to gravitate. They bought good houses, or built well on private land, in order to enjoy the sea air, the lush, alluring countryside. Cottage families were still scattered throughout the hinterland. Some worked in the houses, some laboured on nearby farms and dairies, a few subsisted on local fishing or cockle-gathering.

The atmosphere was predominantly British and Protestant. Monarchists, professional classes, civil servants, officers – their occupations were dictated by their loyalties. The few middle-class Catholics among them were "Castle Catholics", those who by accidents of heritage or education were acceptable at Dublin Castle, the hub of rule. Home Rule and the late Charles Stewart Parnell were permissible conversation – even for ladies. Today all has changed in the natural order which folded Ireland into new shapes after the Anglo-Irish Treaty of 1922. But the change in Sandycove seems to have been slower. Many of the family names persist, the gardens exhibit the continuity, the perennation, of Anglo-Irish gentility in Dublin.

Dinner parties are comfortably hospitable, neighbours are friendly without intrusion, loyalties are more understood than emphasised and Sandycove, calm and neatly arranged, proceeds quietly with its life. Its citizens are solicitors, doctors, retired bankers and superannuated civil servants and there are no demarcation lines along religious grounds. Those Protestant families who flourish will always exercise their Irish franchise, but still take a keen interest in the affairs of the British Royal Family.

With all this gentility was Sandycove not an improbable location for the opening of *Ulysses*? When the novel appeared, on Joyce's fortieth birthday in 1922, there seemed to be only two schools of thought – and criticism. Ford Madox Ford wrote: "One feels admiration that is almost reverence for the incredible labours of this incredible genius." But Alfred Noyes suggested that it was "the foulest book that has ever found its way into print".

Ulysses is an account of ordinary life in a Dublin day on Thursday, June the 16th, 1904. It is a huge, wandering novel, intricate, comic, tragi-comic, explicit, carnal, cloacal. Within its punning idiom a celebrated Dublin punster described it as "more a public labyrinth than a Celtic toilet". Not for nothing did Joyce identify with Dedalus who created the labyrinth, and he scorned, denounced the soft lights of the more romantic Celtic literary twilight.

James Joyce's odyssey begins at the Tower at eight o'clock in the morning when "Stately, plump Buck Mulligan came from the stairhead, bearing a bowl of lather on which a mirror and a razor lay crossed". It ends eighteen jig-sawed hours later, on the far side of Dublin, when Stephen Dedalus has met Leopold Bloom; Telemachus has met his father Ulysses, the young, uncertain Joyce has met the assimilating maturity of the older Joyce – and Molly Bloom says "yes I will yes".

As in much day-to-day life the drama in *Ulysses* is small but incessant. There are disagreements, disappointments, betrayals, jokes, happinesses, hungers, thirsts, birth and death, wages, work and wonder. W. B. Yeats, the poet, called it "the vulgarity of a single Dublin day prolonged to seven hundred pages", an unnecessary and imperceptive disparagement; Joyce believed that the key to human character lay in observing the commonest acts of man. In *Ulysses* he exhibits the city's unremarkable inhabitants, and their commonplace activities are portrayed minutely.

The day Joyce chose was significant. On the 16th of June, 1904 he first walked out with Nora Barnacle, a dark-eyed full-blown woman from the West of Ireland with whom he fell endlessly in love. Was a woman ever so commemorated in literature? And she never even read *Ulysses*!

On the first page Buck Mulligan is shaving in the open air on top of the Tower, when Stephen Dedalus joins him. A conversation occurs in which Mulligan is unspeakably mocking about the death of Stephen's mother, a matter in which Stephen feels substantial guilt. "A light wind passed his brow, fanning softly his fair uncombed hair and stirring silver points of anxiety in his eyes."

Joyce's own mother had died a year before, after a long vomiting illness during which he rejected her wishes that he return to the practice and sacraments of Catholicism. Should Telemachus have listened to his mother, Penelope, and not gone in search of Ulysses, his father? Joyce's reasons for choosing Homer's *Odyssey* for creating his own epic have exercised scholars. It wasn't simply that the mythical wanderings of the Greek hero provided a convenient framework: Ulysses – as he preferred to call Odysseus – seemed to him the complete man in literature, a man who could

THE FORTY FOOT
GENTLEMEN'S
BATHING PLACE
WOMEN
WELCOME
NOT
BRING
DOGS

work his way through the misadventures of life, survive using wisdom and prudence as his only weapons and eventually return to the waiting Penelope.

Joyce divided his own odyssey into eighteen parts and gave them – in his mind and work, although not actually stated in the published book – titles corresponding to people or incidents in Homer's tale. Thus he cast Stephen Dedalus, aged twenty-two as Joyce then was, in the role of Telemachus.

The conversation in the Tower parapet grew even more acrimonius. Mulligan the medical student baited Stephen the poet. "And what is death, he asked, your mother's or yours or my own? You only saw your mother die. I see them pop off every day in the Mater and Richmond and cut up into tripes in the dissecting room." Downstairs Haines the Englishman is waiting and all three breakfast, while an old woman brings them new milk which she obtained "crouching by a patient cow at daybreak in the lush fields". Buck Mulligan wants to drink later; Stephen's wages from a nearby school are thus bespoken.

From the opening page when Buck Mulligan "held the bowl aloft and intoned: *Introibo ad altare Dei*" and mocked the Mass, to the last chapter where Molly Bloom lies languidly and explicitly in her erotic bed, Joyce's flouting of convention gave *Ulysses* a reputation for obscenity which caused litigation, censorship and attempted suppression.

"The most infamously obscene book in ancient or modern literature," *Sunday Express.*

"Our first impression is that of sheer disgust," *Daily Express.*

"Enough to make a Hottentot sick," *Sporting Times.*

Such reviews reflected the general opinion in which *Ulysses* has been held in Ireland. It was denounced and denied and the name James Joyce was a sulphurous cloud. So effective were the book's antagonists that there was no need to ban it – the stain stayed. Which is how I first came to hear the name of James Joyce. Some of my childhood holidays were spent near Dublin, and I first wandered around Sandycove and its Tower with the sons of my uncle. The leader of these cousins kicked the Tower dramatically one day and said it was in a dirty book by a man called Joyce.

Inside the Tower, long before my cousin kicked it, the trio finished their breakfast and Mulligan decided to swim in the Forty-Foot.

"And there's your Latin quarter hat, he said. Stephen picked it up and put it on. Haines called to them from the doorway: Are you coming, you fellows?" Stephen, Mulligan and Haines (who is no more than a scratching-post of a character) left the Tower, wearing, variously, second-hand breeks, stiff collars, rebellious ties, clean handkerchiefs, a primrose waistcoat even, and wandered down between "leader shoots of fern" to the Forty-Foot. The bathing-place is still a male bastion, a curious little place where myriad men sit about in aimless nakedness: a few years ago some heated Hibernian feminists tried to storm it. Mulligan immersed himself, Haines smoked on a rock, Stephen departed, vowing never to visit them again.

The Joycean mischiefs are beginning. Swimming with Mulligan is a young man who flickers much later. He is a student too, with a knowledge of the town of Mullingar and would have, if permitted, a knowledge of a young lady called Milly Bloom. But he merely flickers. With colons and commas, in brush-strokes and little daubs did Joyce portray Dublin – and therefore the world.

Today, James Joyce's Tower is much refined. The "dark, winding stairs" have been whitewashed, symbolically enough. The museum display cases contain Joyce's tie, waistcoat and guitar, some items presented by Samuel Beckett and other friends in literary endowment. Leaflets and pamphlets and booklets bear witness to the intellectual curiosity value of the man who swore that his work would "keep the professors busy for years".

In 1904 the place was shabbier, but today you can still feel Joyce's shade and shape. Tall, thin, aloof, a haughtiness that would grow into arrogance, the thick unwinking spectacles, the clothes shabby, or borrowed, or both, the manner compelling, the demeanour alternating between animation and broody silence. His conversation was always literary and intellectual but his personality was as grubby as his impecuniousness; his inability to get on with

people, and his general disenchantment with Ireland had become apparent early. Was it that Ireland, Dublin, had become too small for him? Yet, he wrote later: "If I can get to the heart of Dublin, I can get to the heart of every city in the world. In the particular is contained the universal". Perhaps he chose, instead, to be the surgeon who prefers not to look upon the face of the patient.

The Tower lingers on the land when you Sealink your way to England. It makes an appropriate point of departure: the incident with Gogarty/Mulligan and Trench/Haines finally convinced James Joyce to leave Ireland and seek silence, exile and cunning.
Unhesitatingly he took with him that red-haired, dark-eyed woman of the 16th of June, Nora Barnacle: "I desire that you should share any happiness that may be mine and to assure you of my great respect for that love of yours which it is my wish to deserve and answer." Joyce never lived in Ireland again and he made few visits. His homes were to be in Trieste, Zurich and Paris. Nora bore him two children and immense love and they finally married in 1931.

"We'll see you again, Haines said, turning as Stephen walked up the path . . ." And the story has begun, the long bell of the day has commenced its ringing. Thursday, the 16th of June, 1904, was a normal, unremarkable Dublin day.

ULSTER

NESTOR

Dalkey, a hilly village, looks calmly and violetly down on Dublin Bay. In 1904, in these hushed and paved leafy avenues, James Joyce filled a temporary vacancy as "a gentleman usher" in an academy for boys.

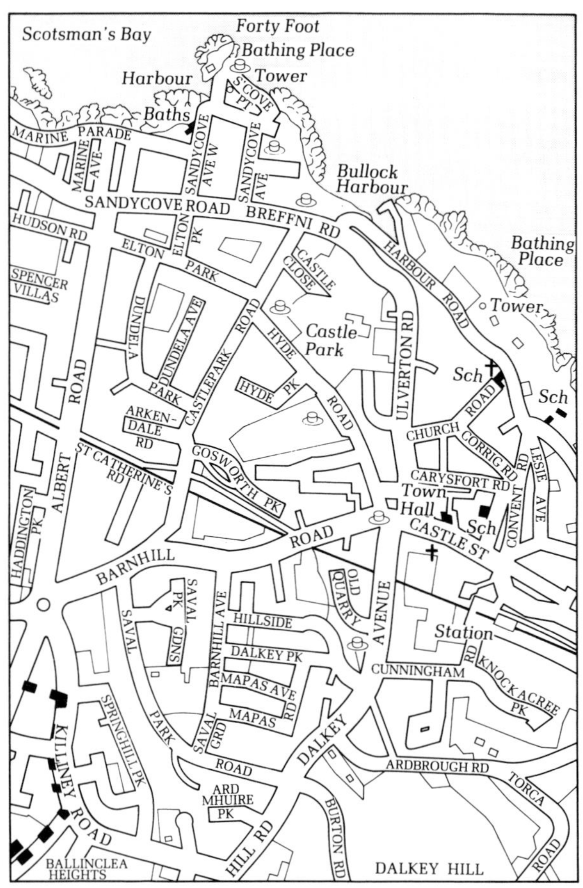

Summerfield Lodge is almost exactly one mile, as the crow flies, from the Martello Tower; and on foot, a distance of a mile and a tenth, a fit quarter of an hour. Stephen walked from Sandycove towards the glistening hill-housed countryside, then as now, bush-cushioned and buttressed, along Sandycove Avenue East and Breffni Road (a continuation of Sandycove Road), past creamy, louvred dwellings. Walk it now and you pass the gap of Bullock Harbour pretending to be a marina, into Ulverton Road where Our Lady's Manor genteels further a gentle home for the geriatric wealthy.

On a June morning in 1904 would an occasional carriage, a lady cyclist in, perhaps, her bloomers, a horseman, have passed Stephen? Now traffic lights stagger the journey. Some of the older houses along Ulverton Road have either been replaced by split-level enclaves, or their speculative demolition has simply left gaps in the gums. At the end of Ulverton Road there is a T-junction and Stephen turned right, ignoring the village of Dalkey, then sharp left up the hill of Dalkey Avenue. At his left hand, shadowed, shriven cottages blinked at him over their half-doors. Why are they empty now? So much of Joycean Dublin has disappeared. Did each character in *Ulysses* bear a wand? In Stephen's time the school was at the rear, and today a kindergarten occupies the same space. Through the branches of the willows the distant bay slides into view like a postcard.

By the time he was twenty-two, Stephen's age, Joyce's mind was a tapestry. He had been educated by the Jesuits, who had taught him "how to arrange things in such a way that they become easy to survey and to judge".

He met them first at six and a half years of age – "half-past-six", as he said – when he went to Clongowes Wood, in County Kildare, still the most eminent boys' school in Ireland. His biographer, Richard Ellmann, describes him as "already a well-behaved, slim little boy in adult company, with a pale face and eyes of the palest blue to lend, when he was not laughing, an impenetrable coolness, an odd self-sufficiency, to otherwise regular and predictable features. His nearsightedness was soon to make him wear

glasses . . ." But his father's eventual and continuous impecuniousness caused young James to be withdrawn from Clongowes after only three years; he spent two more years (which he always chose to forget) in a Christian Brothers school at North Richmond Street in Dublin and finally returned to the Jesuits in Belvedere College, where he remained until he went to University.

University College, Dublin, freed him from the compulsion to keep winning academic prizes and exhibitions at school in order to support the family, whose gentility grew shabbier and shabbier; the vagrant Joyces rented often and often used the banisters as firewood. James left the University in June 1902 with a lazy pass and decided to wade into the literary pool that was then Dublin, with William Butler Yeats, the flowing poet, John Millington Synge the playwright of the Western world, Lady Gregory, the self-appointed patron of the Celtic twilight, George Moore, the elegant bitch and George Russell ("A.E."), bearded, enthusiastic, enigmatic, who arranged the meeting between Joyce and Yeats which gave rise to the story:

"How old are you, Yeats?"

"I am forty."

"Then you are much too old for me to help you. Good day to you."

Apocryphal? Sadly, yes. But Yeats did comment on Joyce's appalling manners, even though he acknowledged the emerging talent.

Stephen was a sympathetic teacher, not a brilliant one. He always identified with the runt.

> "You, Armstrong. Do you know anything about Pyrrhus?"
>
> A bag of figrolls lay snugly in Armstrong's satchel. He curled them between his palms at whiles and swallowed them softly. Crumbs adhered to the tissues of his lips. A sweetened boy's breath. Welloff people, proud that their eldest son was in the navy. Vico Road, Dalkey,
>
> Pyrrhus, sir? Pyrrhus, a pier.
>
> All laughed. Mirthless high malicious laughter.

Dalkey village is not yet dragged into conurbated conformity. The streets, castled and churched, remain much as Stephen saw them along his left shoulder.

Joyce taught a boy who ate figrolls in the Clifton school on Dalkey Avenue in 1904. Stephen taught Roman history and English literature and then prepared himself for a discourse from Mr. Deasy. When Telemachus left the lovely lake of Ocean he stepped ashore to where Nestor, son of Neleus, glory of the Achaean race, sat with his sons and told stories of Trojan battles, voyages and sacrifices of bulls.

Mr. Deasy began to instruct Stephen in the cause of Irish nationalism and in the cure of foot-and-mouth disease in cattle, on which subject he had written a letter to the newspapers which he hoped Stephen might be able, with his literary connections, to have published. Most important, he paid Stephen's wages.

A sovereign fell, bright and new, on the soft pile of the tablecloth.

Three, Mr. Deasy said, turning his little savingsbox about in his hand. These are handy things to have. See. This is for sovereigns. This is for shillings, sixpences, halfcrowns. And here crowns. See.

He shot from it two crowns and two shillings.

Ireland then was at comparative peace. Victoria's calm had reigned. Home Rule was rising, a benign sun, over in the east, towards London. The ivy leaf of Parnell was still mourned. Nationalism meant earnest argument and logical discourse.

Mr. Deasy didn't mince his words:

Old England is dying.

He stepped swiftly off, his eyes coming to blue life as they passed a broad sunbeam. He faced about and back again.

Dying, he said, if not dead by now.

The harlot's cry from street to street
Shall weave old England's winding sheet.

Joyce had had immense difficulty with the Dublin publishers of his short stories, *Dubliners*. The publisher, George Roberts, demanded an amendment to what he considered an unflattering reference to the Queen. "Here's this chap come to the throne after his *old mother* keeping him out of it till the man was grey." Joyce amended it all right. It came back: ". . . his bloody old bitch of a mother . . ."

Quiet, residentially desirable, old-monied, Dalkey

Avenue leads on up into the heights of the hill. At night furtive eyes in the carpark gaze out over the lights of the strumpet city; by day dogs, children and walkers laugh through the groves on the hillside. Stephen Dedalus left that hillside to go to Dublin. "On his wise shoulders through the checkerwork of leaves the sun flung spangles, dancing coins." He is on his way to meet, ineluctably, his father Ulysses. No wonder Joyce was grateful to the Jesuits. "How to arrange things in such a way that they become easy to survey and to judge", indeed. So well did he learn from his teachers and priests that the characters who walk about inside his huge coiling novel even now still create the loudest whisper in the blessed mutter of Dublin's ghosts.

PROTEUS

Sandymount Strand is the palate of Dublin Bay, a horseshoe within a horseshoe, curving, lapping, long. Walkers and wild birds travel the ridged, cockled, herringbone sands.

Two tall red-and-white chimneys mark the Pigeon House power station where the strand begins. Stephen must have taken the Dalkey tram to Haddington Road and there changed for the Sandymount tram to Tritonville Road, thence on foot by way of Leahy's Terrace to Sandymount Strand. In his footsteps today you will observe on one side of the street Massey's funeral parlour faced by (apt juxtaposition) a pub called Cheerio Ryan's, followed by Marie Basquille Confections, next to Brendella Skirts. Proceed, past the huge black hat of the Top Hat Roller Disco Fun For All The Family, which would have appealed to the young Joyce. By the wedding cake of Monkstown Church the Dedalus-bearing tram lurched, on through Blackrock village, through Booterstown, past the house of the tenor John McCormack – with whom Joyce once appeared in a concert – and on by Merrion. Did Stephen pass the brick Bank of Ireland in Ballsbridge where I ledger-clerked for a time and made fiscal history by granting a wayward customer an overdraft on his deposit account?

Certainly he passed by the grounds of the Royal Dublin Society and crossed Ball's Bridge over the Dodder River. Today the red roads of Ballsbridge, originally wide to let old regiments march through ceremonially, are interspersed with hotels never then intended, and the American Embassy, circular in design to commemorate the shape of the old Irish fort. The last lap of Stephen's journey to Sandymount is still a dribbling, nondescript passageway along streets of small houses to the sea.

I know a man who changed his name to protect this view of Dublin Bay. When Sandymount and its environs received notice of an impending oil refinery, he inserted the words "Dublin" and "Bay" between the words "Sean" and "Loftus", in order to get the issue named on the actual ballot paper when he was running for local office – a deed for the poll. He won both the election and the battle: there is no refinery.

At about eleven o'clock in the morning Stephen came to Sandymount – to think. "Proteus" is the first chapter in *Ulysses* in which Joyce makes extensive use of the device for which the novel became famous, the stream of consciousness, the *monologue interieur.* Many have parodied it since, none have accomplished it so brilliantly.

Are the opening words of "Proteus" James Joyce's keyboard? "Ineluctable modality of the visible, at least that, if no more, thought through my eyes", the towering phrase, the shining phrase of *Ulysses* sits grave and beautiful inside Stephen's head.

Ineluctable, *adj.*, that cannot be escaped from.

Modality, *n.*, the quality of being limited by a condition.

Sandymount Strand, ineluctable as sin, sweeps wide and grey and beige, stippled with gulls and aeroplanes and lighthouses and ships and lone Dedalus-walkers. "Signatures of all things I am here to read, seaspawn and seawrack, the nearing tide, that rusty boot." Most of the thoughts in Stephen's mind as he walked along Sandymount Strand were triggered by that ineluctable modality of the visible.

First he sees two worthy ladies from the Liberties of Dublin, "the two maries", out for the day, one of them carrying a midwife's bag. "What has she in the bag? A misbirth with a trailing navelcord, hushed in ruddy wool. The cord of all link back, strandentwining cable of all flesh", and Stephen fantasises that it might be possible, using this umbilical telephone line, to dial back to Adam and Eve. Then his mind wanders back and forth over his life so far, like a lazy sieve, recalling family incidents and persons. "In his broad bed nuncle Richie, pillowed and blanketed, extends over the hillock of his knees a sturdy forearm. Cleanchested. He has washed the upper moiety."

Stephen recalls incidents at school. "You told the Clongowes gentry you had an uncle a judge and an uncle a general in the army." Stephen reviews the religious and irreligious fits he used to have, all woman-inspired. "You were awfully holy, weren't you? You prayed to the Blessed Virgin that you might not have a red nose. You prayed to the devil in Serpentine Avenue that the fubsy widow in front might lift her clothes still more from the wet street."

"Ineluctable modality of the visible" was the phrase which ensured that *Ulysses* would first be published. The novel originally appeared, not in book form, but by instalment. *The Little Review*, an American publication, was run by two ladies who were interested in avant-garde prose. They deserve to be named – Margaret Anderson and Jane Heap; the intermediary between them and James Joyce was the poet Ezra Pound. When the two ladies read the ineluctable modality they immediately became daughters of a literary revolution and there and then declared their willingness to lay down their lives for *Ulysses* and its author.

Stephen Dedalus on Sandymount Strand was a troubled young man. The green mucous sea and Mulligan's sickening mockery had reminded him of his mother's illness and vomiting death. His failure to grant her dying wish and return to Catholicism has haunted him and, he knows, always will. So, there he was walking across the sands of Sandymount, a pale, blue-eyed, fair-haired young man, thin but too fine to be gaunt, with an aloofness that will yet be ascetic.

> The grainy sand had gone from under his feet. His boots trod again a damp, crackling mast, razorshells, squeaking pebbles, that on the unnumbered pebbles beats, wood sieved by the shipworm, lost Armada. Unwholesome sandflats waited to suck his treading soles, breathing upward sewage breath. He coasted them, walking warily. A porter-bottle stood up, stogged to its waist, in the cakey sand dough.

Nothing changes – except that they didn't have Coke tins and Polystyrene in 1904. Of the early parts of *Ulysses* the episode which pleased Joyce most was "Proteus". Even though Stephen wasn't an old man and didn't emerge from the waves, he still changed form. From being dull, sullen, listless and bitter he relaxed, became easy with himself, cheerful. And all around him the strand was changing with the tide, the landscape was changing with people wandering in and out of view, the sky was changing with clouds across it.

"His feet marched in sudden proud rhythm over the sand furrows, along by the boulders of the south wall. He stared at them proudly, piled stone mammoth skulls. Gold light on sea, on sand, on boulders. The sun is there, the slender trees, the lemon houses." Sandymount Strand still takes on a light you find further south in Europe, a cinnnamon-and-water light, I've seen it in towns near Rome, in villages near Marseilles, by shores where the Mediterranean stands still with thick, sickening pollution. In the Sandymount distance, to the south, three half-hearted hills; by the road, the railway line, Victorian terraces of houses, a shard of glassed architecture, sparse trees.

"He had come nearer the edge of the sea and wet sand slapped his boots. The new air greeted him, harping in wild nerves, wind of wild air of seeds of brightness." Each night six reliable lighthouses finger this shore with their gentle, yellow insistence.

Stephen saw a dead dog, then a live one, thought of panthers. Stephen mused on the man who was "drowned nine days ago off Maiden's Rock". Would his body float up, white-bloated? Stephen observed: "A woman and a man. I see her skirties. Pinned up, I bet." Stephen dreamed of a dead friend, a dynamitard in Paris, and of a girl he tried to pick up, he dreamed of corpses and ghosts, of longlashed eyes, of shells. He lay on the rocks at Sandymount Strand waiting for Proteus to come up from the sea and change all things. Over his shoulder "moving through the air high spars of a threemaster, her sails brailed up on the crosstrees, homing, upstream, silently moving, a silent ship".

CALYPSO

At eight o'clock on the morning of 16th of June, 1904, Mr. Leopold Bloom stepped out on the doorstep of Number Seven, Eccles Street, Dublin. As he stood beneath the lintel, drawing the door softly closed behind him, sunbeams glanced at the steeple of Saint George's Church.

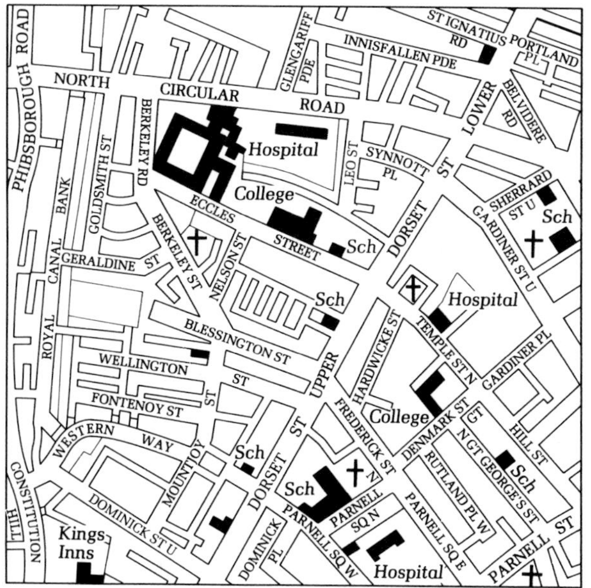

Mr. Bloom and his wife Molly lived quite near the Dorset Street corner of Eccles Street. At the other end Buck Mulligan in the Mater Misericordiae Hospital saw people every day "cut into tripes in the dissecting room". Eccles Street was part of the Georgian organisation of Dublin, and on the face of it now, a wrinkled, nondescript face, Eccles Street seems a curious choice for one of the most famous addresses in literature. But Joyce always had his reasons. Just as he chose the single day of *Ulysses* to commemorate Nora's arrival in his life, he gave Bloom an address which would also commemorate her.

According to Joyce's researches in *Thom's Directory* Number Seven, Eccles Street was vacant on the 16th of June, 1904: later it was to be the home of his great and good friend J. F. Byrne. On a brief return to Ireland in 1909, long before he began to write *Ulysses*, Joyce spent pleasant hours in conversation there but one afternoon, when he called to see Byrne, he was in a state of great misery.

Dublin is, always has been, a jealous city; metaphorically your throat may be cut while your back is turned. Joyce's genius, accompanying arrogance and cool, superior manner irritated his less talented "friends". One of these, an indolent called Cosgrave, told the holidaying Joyce that Nora had not, originally, been as faithful as she pretended. Cosgrave had once been an unsuccessful rival for Nora's attentions and now he informed Joyce that he had, in fact, been clandestinely successful, that when Joyce understood she was working late Cosgrave had been dallying with her. He may have hinted leeringly at sexual connexion too, "carnival knowledge" Dublin calls it.

Joyce was shattered. Even though his masochistic psyche had always needed moral martyrdom, this was terrible. A most tearful, pathetic letter was dashed off to Nora in Trieste:

> I have heard this only an hour ago from his lips. My eyes are full of tears, tears of sorrow and mortification. My heart is full of bitterness and

despair. I can see nothing but your face as it was then raised to meet another's. O, Nora, pity me for what I suffer now. I shall cry for days. My faith in that face I loved is broken. O, Nora, Nora, have pity for my poor wretched love. I cannot call you any dear name because tonight I have learned that the only being I believed in was not loyal to me.

The following morning at dawn, after a night of dark and anguish, he wrote again: "O Nora! Nora! Nora! I am speaking now to the girl I loved, who had red-brown hair and sauntered over to me and took me so easily into her arms and made me a man." Like a spirit possessed – which he was, by sorrow – he wandered, aimless and strained, around Dublin. Finally, two days after the awful information, he went to Number Seven, Eccles Street to confide in Byrne whom he trusted.

Byrne rallied and railed. Unlike Joyce, he hadn't left Dublin and had kept pace with the city's sense of jealousy and conspiracy. He soon smelt what had happened, that the story of Nora's infidelity was in fact a vengeful plan hatched by the envious Cosgrave and viciously encouraged by Gogarty. Subsequently Nora – who had behaved quietly and with dignity under such swingeing accusations – confided in Joyce's brother, Stanislaus, who was able to confirm Byrne's assessment. Cosgrave had previously admitted to Stanislaus his failure to oust Joyce from Nora's heart. It was never difficult to convince Joyce that people were conspiring against him and his relief was so complete that he commemorated Nora's fidelity by immortalising Number Seven, Eccles Street.

Dublin wakes slowly and mistily; the spires step forward from the mountains, the smoke carries the smell of fresh bread. "Mr. Leopold Bloom ate with relish the inner organs of beasts and fowls." When

Mr. Bloom appears in *Ulysses* for the first time, in the "Calypso" episode, he is preparing for a universally common experience, breakfast. "Kidneys were in his mind as he moved about the kitchen softly, righting her breakfast things on the humpy tray. Gelid light and air were in the kitchen but out of doors gentle summer morning everywhere. Made him feel a bit peckish."

Leopold Bloom is thirty-eight years old, and is descended from a Hungarian Jew. His father, Rudolph Virag, was fifty-nine when Leopold was born and had arrived in Ireland the previous year. Leopold's mother was Ellen Higgins, their only child was born in Clanbrassil Street, the Jewish area of Dublin, on the 6th of May, 1866. Joyce polished his verisimilitude until you could see his character's face in it.

"He heard then a warm heavy sigh, softer, as she turned over and the loose brass quoits of the bedstead jingled." (As they do in a recurring timpany throughout the novel.) Molly Bloom is lying in bed not yet fully awake. Dark-haired, wilful, plain-spoken, almost thirty-four years old, Mrs. Marion Bloom (neé Tweedy) is bountifully constructed. The daughter of a British soldier in Gibraltar and a girl of Spanish blood named Lunita Laredo – though there are doubts about both parentages – Molly Bloom's is the scent which stays in the nostrils of the entire novel, from the moment Mr. Bloom "pulled the halldoor to after him very quietly, more, till the footleaf dropped gently over the threshold, a limp lid".

Servants were about their employers' business as Mr Bloom walked to the corner of Eccles Street and Dorset Street, turned right past Larry O'Rourke's pub, to Dlugacz's meat shop. "His hand accepted the moist tender gland and slid it into a side-pocket." Threepence for the kidney for his breakfast and Mr. Bloom walks back along Dorset Street, reading from the piece of paper the meat-shop man used as wrapping paper. Larry O'Rourke's pub, under different ownership now, is still licensed to sell beer, wine and spirits but do not go looking for moist tender glands on Dorset Street, at least not in meat-shops: Dlugacz's is one of the few fictional addresses in *Ulysses*.

"A cloud began to cover the sun wholly slowly wholly", the same cloud that Stephen Dedalus, far away on the other side of the city, has seen "shadowing the bay in deeper green". Once, in this part of Dublin I trysted with a girl who, like me, had no timepiece, but we both lived in earshot, though in opposite directions, of the same church. So we left our separate residences when the bell began to ring. Thus, later, and through the entire day, the same bells ring in the ears of different characters in *Ulysses*, the same processions are saluted in different parts of the city, the same persons are observed in different streets.

Now, as Stephen Dedalus is massaging his chagrin at Buck Mulligan, Mr. Bloom is entering his hallway, and taking an anxious breath. On the floor, among the letters is one to his wife, addressing her as "Mrs. Marion Bloom"; she uses "Marion" when singing in popular concerts. The letter is from Blazes Boylan, the flash, straw-hatted, thuggish impresario who is cuckolding Bloom crudely and laughingly. Having already established him as the irreverent, insensitive Buck Mulligan, Joyce made it clear that Oliver St. John Gogarty was (spectrally at least) Blazes Boylan also – revenge to the full.

Letters in hand, "Entering the bedroom he half-closed his eyes and walked through the warm yellow twilight towards her tousled head." Molly, to whom Joyce's Bloom is as enslaved as Homer's Ulysses was to Queenly Calypso, lies there, on her island too: "She set the brasses jingling as she raised herself briskly, an elbow on the pillow."

He brings her "bread and butter, four, sugar, spoon, her cream" and explains that "metempsychosis", which she has just come across in her reading, means the transmigration of souls. "The warmth of her couched body rose on the air, mingling with the fragrance of the tea she poured." Suddenly, gently, you can feel the air around Mr Bloom grow heavy with sadness because of Blazes Boylan's letter. Down in the kitchen Mr Bloom finishes the cooking of the kidney and sits down to his own breakfast. Breakfast. What other meal could be so appropriate to begin the odyssey of Mr. Bloom? As dawn came with rosy fingers did not Calypso feed Ulysses before he sailed on the wine-dark seas away from her enchanted island?

Mr. Bloom reads a letter from his daughter, fifteen-year-old Milly in Mullingar, where she is working as a photographer's assistant and has taken a shine to a student called Bannon. Mr. Bloom ponders mildly the failures of his life: the death of their baby Rudy unsettled the sexual possibilities between him and Molly, and Blazes Boylan is going to call and see her later that day. But if Mr. Bloom cannot get his house in order he can at least get his body in order and after a "gentle loosening of his bowels" he leaves the house. The clock strikes a quarter to nine; Mr. Bloom is dressed darkly, because he is on his way to the funeral of poor Dignam. On the other side of the city Stephen has already heard a clock striking a quarter to nine; the long day's journey into night which will bring together Ulysses and Telemachus, Mr. Bloom and Stephen Dedalus, has begun. Mr. Leopold Bloom has had his breakfast and Mr. James Joyce has had his joke, a Jew breaking the fast from midnight before going forth to a multifarious communion.

Eccles Street is a quiet street now, the red brick is blackened, Mr. Bloom's house no more than an empty socket. You can still taste vicariously the genteel grandeur it once enjoyed: fanlights and

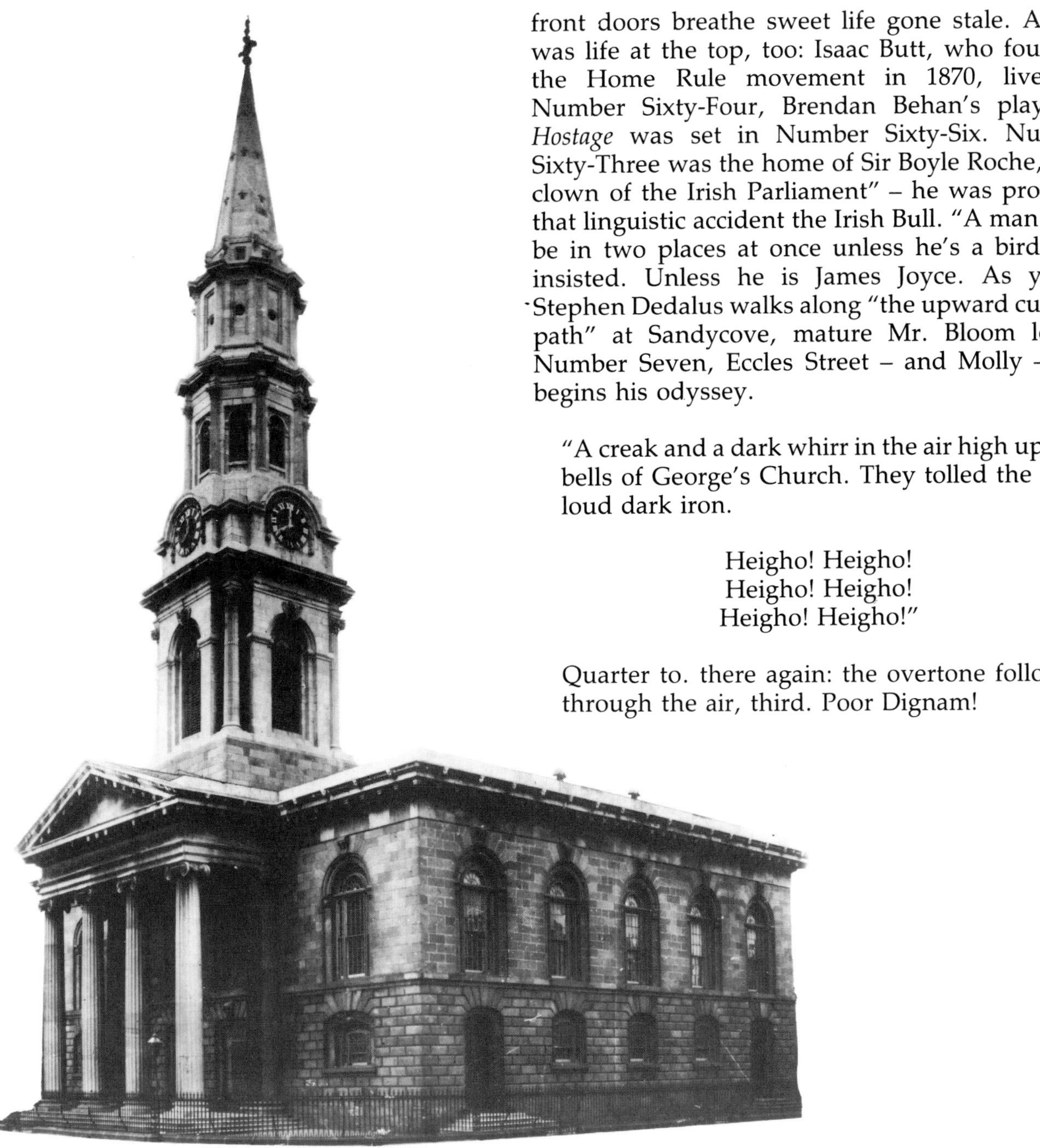

front doors breathe sweet life gone stale. And it was life at the top, too: Isaac Butt, who founded the Home Rule movement in 1870, lived at Number Sixty-Four, Brendan Behan's play *The Hostage* was set in Number Sixty-Six. Number Sixty-Three was the home of Sir Boyle Roche, "the clown of the Irish Parliament" – he was prone to that linguistic accident the Irish Bull. "A man can't be in two places at once unless he's a bird," he insisted. Unless he is James Joyce. As young Stephen Dedalus walks along "the upward curving path" at Sandycove, mature Mr. Bloom leaves Number Seven, Eccles Street – and Molly – and begins his odyssey.

> "A creak and a dark whirr in the air high up. The bells of George's Church. They tolled the hour: loud dark iron.
>
> Heigho! Heigho!
> Heigho! Heigho!
> Heigho! Heigho!"
>
> Quarter to. there again: the overtone following through the air, third. Poor Dignam!

LOTUS EATERS

Swans, sweepstakes, gunboats, Guinness, all have floated on the narrow green tide of the River Liffey, Anna Livia Plurabelle, Dublin's own stream of consciousness. Three hundred yards wide once, it formed a dark pool, the Dubh Linn of the Vikings.

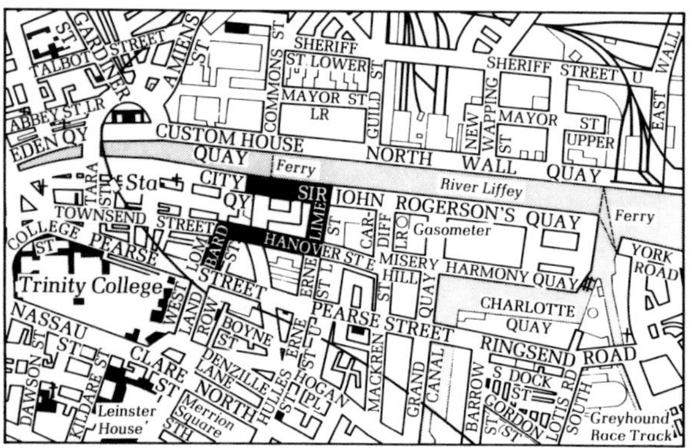

If you leave Number Seven, Eccles Street, cross Dorset Street and walk past St. George's Church, down the sloping streets towards the Liffey, you walk through a part of Dublin that has had a long day's dying. The houses are going, are gone, and the people with them. Corners boarded up, walls sloganed, skeletal tenements stalk you. On the street corners, erupting from behind the red traffic lights, thieves break car windows, snatch bags and disappear into the shadowed tenement tunnels.

Dublin is divided by the Liffey as a great house was divided by the staircase. Those "below stairs" were said to live on the North side, the grander folk on the south side. When Joyce's foe, Gogarty, escaped a Civil War execution by swimming across the Liffey he gave thanks later by bestowing on the river a gift of swans. Mindful of the sewage bobbing near his head, he subsequently described his escapade as "going through the motions". The Irish Hospital Sweepstakes launched exotic advertising campaigns on the Liffey. As one self-important Guinness skipper negotiated his barge the few hundred yards under the low bridges to the waiting ship a wag on a parapet yelled: "Hey, Mister – bring us back a parrot!"

Mr. Bloom's Thursday morning journey has an exotic intoxicating purpose too. Further to his enquiry – a discreet newspaper advertisement, actually – he has been engaged in a randy clandestine correspondence with a lady called Martha in the far south-western suburb of Dolphin's Barn. His post restante address is c/o Westland Row Post Office, his pen name is Henry Flower and he is expecting a letter. "By lorries along Sir John Rogerson's Quay Mr. Bloom walked soberly, past Windmill Lane, Leask's the linseed crushers, the postal telegraph office." He turned right and south into Lime Street, right again along Hanover Street to turn left into Lombard Street. Then he walked along Lombard Street, crossed Great Brunswick Street (now Pearse Street) and into Westland Row.

He could have approached Westland Row by a much more direct route; he didn't need to go down the quays as far as Lime Street and then turn back. But his conscience interrogated him about this naughty letter – and he did not want to bump into any friends or acquaintances who might accompany him and discover his purpose, thus he took a devious route. And if you trace Mr. Bloom's steps from the quayside to the post office, you will find that it describes a huge question mark – which must have been deliberate on Joyce's part, since he measured his characters' movements with a ruler, compass and stop-watch.

As Mr. Bloom crossed the Liffey and walked parallel to the river the Custom House sat on the river, watching him, busier then; the ships dock further down now. The architect, James Gandon, wore his sword to the Custom House building site to protect himself from the hostilities of the merchants – who feared it would reduce upriver trading – of the neighbours, who worried that the building would attract "a low and vulgar crowd with the manners of Billingsgate". Ten years build-

THE GROSVENOR
HOTEL - LOUNGE - GRILL - BAR
GROSVENOR
LENWOOD
CASH & CARRY
MOTOR ACCESSORIES ETC.
TRADE ONLY
THE BLADES
STARDUST
MON 8th

ing, 1781 to 1791, half a million pounds and Gandon was a Palladian hero. The Custom House is the grace of Dublin, and the riverine gods, whose corniced faces adorn the façade, brought art and commerce together when they were chosen to appear on the Irish banknotes.

Dublin in 1904 was hardly the land of the lotus eaters but, nonetheless, Mr Bloom is lotus eating, prompted principally by the prospect of a letter from Martha, prompted too by the yellow light of the morning, by the sounds of the shining, sluggish river, by the sensation of a digesting breakfast. Mr. Bloom takes off his hat and inhales his own hairoil. Joyce piles on the lotus-eating images. In a shop window, tea from Ceylon evokes the Far East. "Lovely spot it must be: the garden of the world, big lazy leaves to float about on, cactuses, flowery meads, snaky lianas they call them" and on to waterlilies, tired petals, roseleaves until finally contemplating the bath he is about to take, Mr. Bloom recalls "the chap I saw in that picture somewhere? Ah, in the dead sea, floating on his bank, reading a book with a parasol open."

At the post office "he handed the card through the brass grill. Are there any letters for me? he asked." And Henry Flower receives a letter full of promise. (The Hungarian "Virag", Bloom's father's name before he changed it by deed poll, means "flower".)

As well as having a Homeric counterpart, Joyce intended each chapter in *Ulysses* to represent an organ of the body; thus the kidney, for Mr. Bloom's breakfast. In "Lotus Eaters" Joyce displays the genitals. He used symbols; a newspaper rolled "lengthwise in a baton"; suggestions: "you darling manflower"; comment: "an army half-rotten with venereal disease". Now, in early heat, before he can read his letter, an acquaintance accosts him. "Hello, Bloom. Where are you off to? Hello, M'Coy. Nowhere in particular", and Mr. Bloom manages to prevent M'Coy from borrowing a leather valise, "capped corners, riveted edges, double action lever lock". Mr Bloom is too polite to show his impatience but he feels from fingering the letter in his pocket that Martha has sent him something, "A photo it isn't. A badge maybe."

Across the road, a horse-drawn vehicle, an "outsider" by the Grosvenor Hotel, a sleek woman waits to climb aboard. "Stylish kind of coat with that roll collar, warm for a day like this, looks like blanketcloth. Careless stand of her with her hands in those patch pockets. Like that haughty creature at the polo match." A passing tram foils Mr. Bloom's view of the climbing "silk flash rich stockings white". Mr. Bloom feels excluded. Today the Grosvenor Hotel is locked, barred and boarded, a reduced direlict, rattled by high heedless trains crossing the bridge at first-floor level. Mr. Bloom and M'Coy part with talk of poor Dignam who is about to be buried and for whom Mr. Bloom has dressed in black.

From the corner of Great Brunswick Street Mr. Bloom turns right and immediately right again. Mr. Bloom stands on the dingy cobbles soaking in the scent of the illicit flower – containing letter. The lotus blooms below the barren peak – and by every winding creek – but it is all in the mind of Mr. Bloom, dreams of domination, hazy, lazy, dreaming dreams of exotic Martha who has sent him a, and who will open to him like a, flower.

James Joyce based Leopold Bloom on Alfred Hunter, a good Samaritan. Joyce's affair with Nora, six days young, had not as yet gelled, and on the 22nd of June, 1904, the bold James, never backward in coming forward, approached a girl who was merely taking the air. She was already vigorously escorted, so Joyce's nose was out of joint – and bloodied. Alfred Hunter, a Dublin Jew with a straying wife, chanced by, comforted Joyce and bound his wounds. But there is more to Bloom than just Hunter's kindness. Joyce admired the Jews because they chose isolation and because they maintained the closest family ties, qualities evident and abundant in the man himself.

Under the archway Mr. Bloom tears up the envelope, scattering the petals of Henry Flower. Mr. Bloom, a Jew by race, a Christian by conversion, goes to "the backdoor of All Hallows", the Catholic Church on Westland Row, where the "cold smell of sacred stone called him". Why a Jew? Joyce believed that a Jew was king and priest in his own house.

The lotus eating Mr. Bloom kneels to eucharist and incense and contemplates wine. "Makes it more aristocratic than for example if he drank what they are used to Guinness's porter or some temperance beverage Wheatley's Dublin hop bitters or Cantrell and Cochrane's ginger ale (aromatic)."

Mr. Bloom stands a moment "unseeing by the cold black marble bowl while before him and behind two worshippers dipped furtive hands in the low tide of holy water". Intoned a television commentator once as the camera panned across bowed heads and yellow flickering candles: "Whenever I hear of an Irishman losing the faith I hear the cock crow thrice."

Westland Row was the birthplace of two distinguished and elegant institutions. Twenty years apart, both occasioned remarkable comment, initiated new styles of things, and eventually suffered decrepitude to varying degrees. One was the Dublin to Kingstown railway line, born at Westland Row Station in 1834, the other was Oscar Fingal

O'Flahertie Wills Wilde, born at Number Twenty-One, Westland Row, in 1854.

Mr. Bloom turns left from the Church door and walks along Westland Row to Sweny the chemist, to purchase for Molly a facial lotion of "sweet almond oil and tincture of benzoin", and orangeflower water and then a cake of soap for himself of a sweet lemony wax. Outside he meets Bantam Lyons who is lurking for a tip for the Gold Cup to be run that afternoon. Mr. Bloom says that he is just about to throw away his newspaper. "Throwaway" is the name of a horse in the race and Bantam Lyons mistakes Mr. Bloom's generosity for a nod and a wink. But not so – Mr. Bloom is too prudent to gamble and anyway he has other things on his mind. He walks cheerfully towards the baths. "Remind you of a mosque, redbaked bricks, the minarets."

Lotus eating, this is my body eucharist taking, and in the stream the long-leaved flowers weep and from the craggy ledge the poppy hangs in sleep. He lies quiet, dazed and dreamy. He observes his navel, "bud of flesh", and watches the dark "tangled curls of his bush floating, floating hair of the stream around the limp father of thousands, a languid floating flower". All the aromas, the scents, the spiced vapours of early-morning Dublin have been released. He lies in the bath, "naked, in a womb of warmth, oiled by scented melting soap, softly laved". Homer, Christ, Tennyson, Joyce, meet on the page, in the mind.

It is cricket weather. It is the day of the Sports in Trinity College Park (where "Captain Buller broke a window in the Kildare Street Club with a slog to square leg" – so much for W. G. Grace). It is Bloom's day.

HADES

Like the ribboned silver spoor of a snail the funeral path of poor Dignam curled and trailed in the passages of the city. While his soul flew upwards plumed hearse-horses drew his body downwards to Joyce's Hades – the alabaster groves of Glasnevin cemetery.

Even the carriages had a tombstone smell. Buttoned, cracked leather, blinds, top-hatted coachmen – and at the end of it all acres of stilled marbles, heavy-lidded unseeing memorials.

Martin Cunningham, first, poked his silkhatted head into the carriage and, entering deftly, seated himself. Mr. Power stepped in after him, curving his height with care.
Come on, Simon.
After you, Mr. Bloom said.
Mr. Dedalus covered himself quickly and got in.

Poor Dignam, who died from drink-induced apoplexy, lived at Number Nine, Newbridge Avenue, Sandymount, near where Stephen Dedalus is crackling his boots across the seawrack and shells. The grave in Glasnevin is at the very far side of the city. "What way is he taking us? Mr. Power asked through both windows. Irishtown, Martin Cunningham said. Ringsend, Brunswick Street." The journey to Hades begins, a clipping pace in clopping, swaying, creaking carriages.
"All watched awhile through their windows caps and hats lifted by passers. Respect. The carriage swerved from the tramtrack to the smoother road past Watery Lane. Mr. Bloom at gaze saw a lithe young man, clad in mourning, a wide hat": the first epiphany of Stephen and Mr. Bloom. And during a funeral procession? O, Joyce! From January to April, 1903, James Joyce lounged around Paris, cadging subsistence by visiting friends at mealtimes, borrowing money from everybody he could touch. He inhabited libraries, brothels, and cafés: he drank absinthe, met literati and stayed in a small room at the Hotel Corneille in the Latin Quarter (where he bought a hat). On Saturday, the 11th of April, he received a telegram: "Mother dying. Come home. Father." Mr. Joyce left Paris.
May Murray Joyce spent a long time dying, that kindly, concerned, gentle woman. She lay in bed vomiting cancer. She begged her Jim to turn back to the sacraments of the Church. Otherwise tender and yielding, he sang Yeats to her:

Who will go drive with Fergus now,
And pierce the deep wood's woven shade,
And dance upon the level shore?
Young man, lift up your russet brow,
And lift your tender eyelids, maid
And brood on hopes and fear no more.

His hair was long, his bow tie floppy, a small beard straggled across his uneasy face. He wrote little, drank to ease his mother's pain, refused to kneel in prayer by her dying coma. She died in August, he dressed all in Hamlet-black and sat on the staircase, his arm around his alarmed nine-year-old sister, Mabel, advising her not to cry. His mother's forty-four-year-old body was buried in Glasnevin.

"They went past the bleak pulpit of Saint Mark's, under the railway bridge, past the Queen's Theatre: in silence. Hoardings." How to see the great and small streets of Dublin? Follow poor Dignam to Hades. Great Brunswick Street, where Mr. Bloom has earlier stood, now Pearse Street, is still derelict of character. On opposite corners a bank and anonymous shops, then a cinema once the Antient Concert Rooms (sic) incongruously beside St. Mark's Parish Church, whose bleak pulpit was made from the poop of a ship wrecked in the bay: wherein Oscar etc. Wilde was baptised: over which the railway bridge uglily services Westland Row Station.

The street promises to improve, but nothing comes of it – extensions of Trinity College, drab commercial offices, a lone pub, engineering companies and a plaque at Number Twenty-Seven to commemorate the Pearse Brothers, Patrick and Willie, who died in the Poets' Rising of 1916. Junctions now begin to take life away from the street; the Fire Station at Tara Street with its Florentine spire is younger than Mr. Bloom, on the left a block of offices supplanted the Queen's

Theatre of Variety where the Abbey Theatre lodged from 1951 to 1966, until its phoenix rose again across the river.

"Mr. Dedalus bent across to salute. From the door of the Red Bank a white disc of a straw hat flashed reply: passed." It is impossible now for a funeral to go straight from Pearse Street into D'Olier Street. It is just as impossible for a Blazes Boylan to tip his hat outside the Red Bank Restaurant. D'Olier Street is one-way in the other direction: so is the Red Bank – it is a church.

In Paris, James Joyce told Arthur Power, a young Dublin renaissance man, that *Ulysses* was the book of his maturity, which he preferred to his violent and painful youth.

Power replied with a motto he had seen on the dial of an Italian clock: "Every one hurts and the last one kills." Joyce liked it – time as a further ineluctable modality, another key. "We are going the pace, I think, Martin Cunningham said. God grant he doesn't upset us on the road, Mr. Power said." When *Ulysses* first became available in Dublin one asked another: "Am I in it?" Peter-like, a former associate denied all knowledge, ever, of Joyce. "But you're in *Ulysses*," said the journalist. "I am not a character in fiction. I am a living human being." Martin Cunningham was based on a friend of Joyce's father, the bearded Matthew Kane. Mr. Power was Tom Devan, who espied the farewelling Jim and Nora come clandestinely together after they boarded ship and told John Joyce his son hadn't gone alone. Simon Dedalus is John Joyce, a Corkman whose tidal fortunes receded permanently, who sang, sported, drank and married above himself. His firstborn, like Mr. Bloom's, didn't survive, nine of the ten children felt hostile to him, James, his living oldest, adored him, emulated him in music, passion for gossipy detail and penury, tried to commemorate him in stone, set-

HOTEL METROPOLE. SACKVILLE ST. DUBLIN. 4018. W.

tled for prose. In *A Portrait of the Artist as a Young Man*

> Stephen began to enumerate glibly his father's attributes. A medical student, an oarsman, a tenor, an amateur actor, a shouting politician, a small landlord, a small investor, a drinker, a good fellow, a story-teller, somebody's secretary, something in a distillery, a tax-gatherer, a bankrupt, and at present a raiser of his own past.

Undoubtedly John Joyce was the inspiration for many of his son's expressions. Old argot, half-forgotten soldier's words, cliches from penny ballads, sudden truths glinted in his conversation – his ear for music listened to him speaking.

"Oot: a dullgarbed old man from the curbstone tendered his wares, his mouth opening: oot. Four bootlaces for a penny." From D'Olier Street, named for a Huguenot called Jeremiah of the family of Olier; Mr. Cunningham, Mr. Power, Mr. Dedalus and Mr. Bloom corteged over O'Connell Bridge, named for a talking, hunting, arguing, laughing, womanising advocate from Kerry.

Daniel O'Connell, fighting the Act of Union which in 1800 manacled Ireland to England, said that Pitt the Prime Minister had a smile "like the brass plate on a coffin".

"They passed the hugecloaked Liberator's form." Daniel O'Connell, the Liberator, died on his sad, broken way to Rome. In keeping with his beliefs, activities and instincts his heart went to Rome, his body to Glasnevin, his genitals to his native Kerry.

Mr. Cunningham, Mr. Power, Mr. Dedalus and Mr. Bloom sat in the carriage and peeped out at the world moving slowly by. Sackville Street, now O'Connell Street, furlonged ahead.

Tritonville Road, Ringsend Road, Pearse Street, D'Olier Street, O'Connell Street, Parnell Square, Blessington Street, Berkeley Road, North Circular Road, Phibsborough Road, Prospect Road, Finglas Road – a postman's chorus.

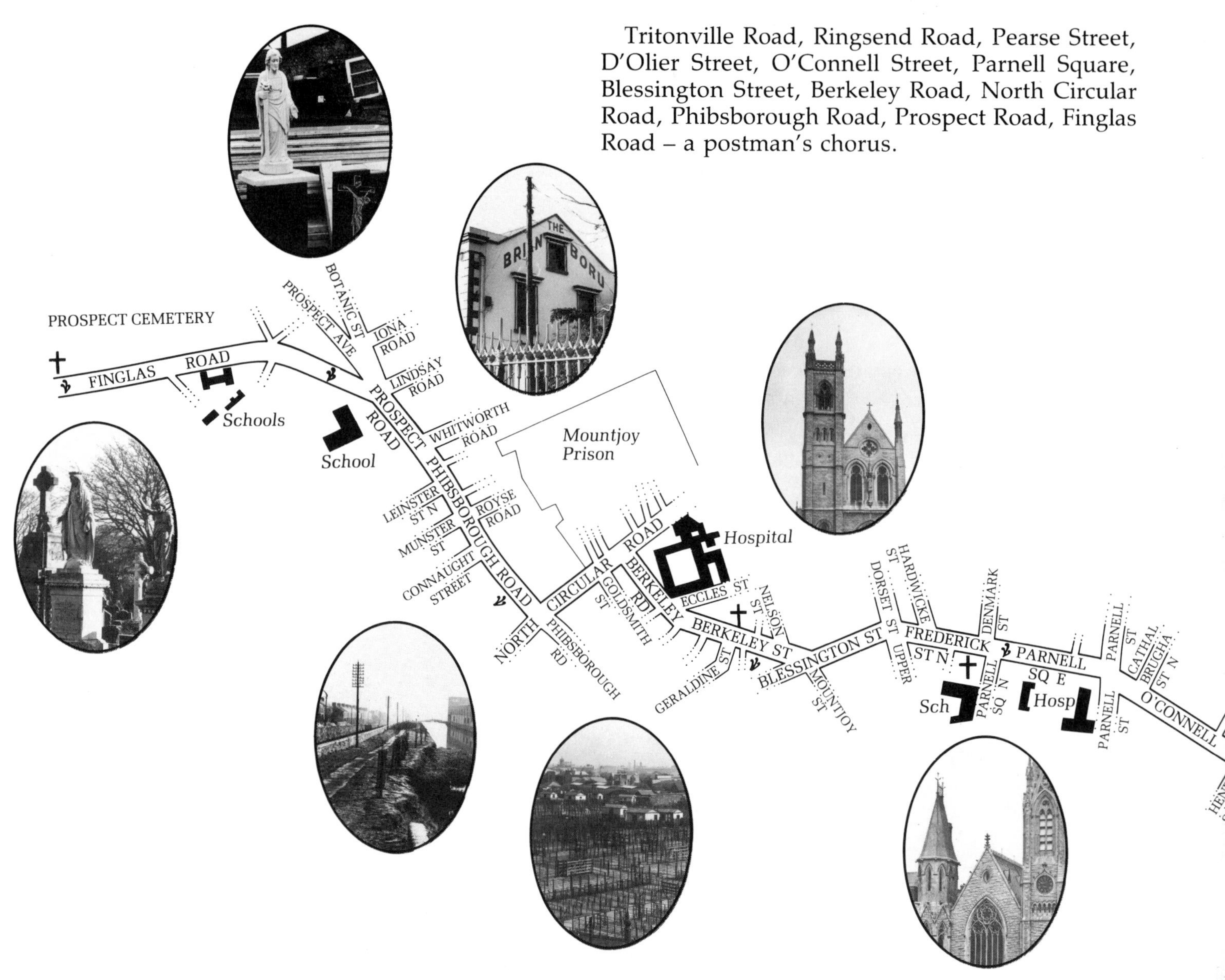

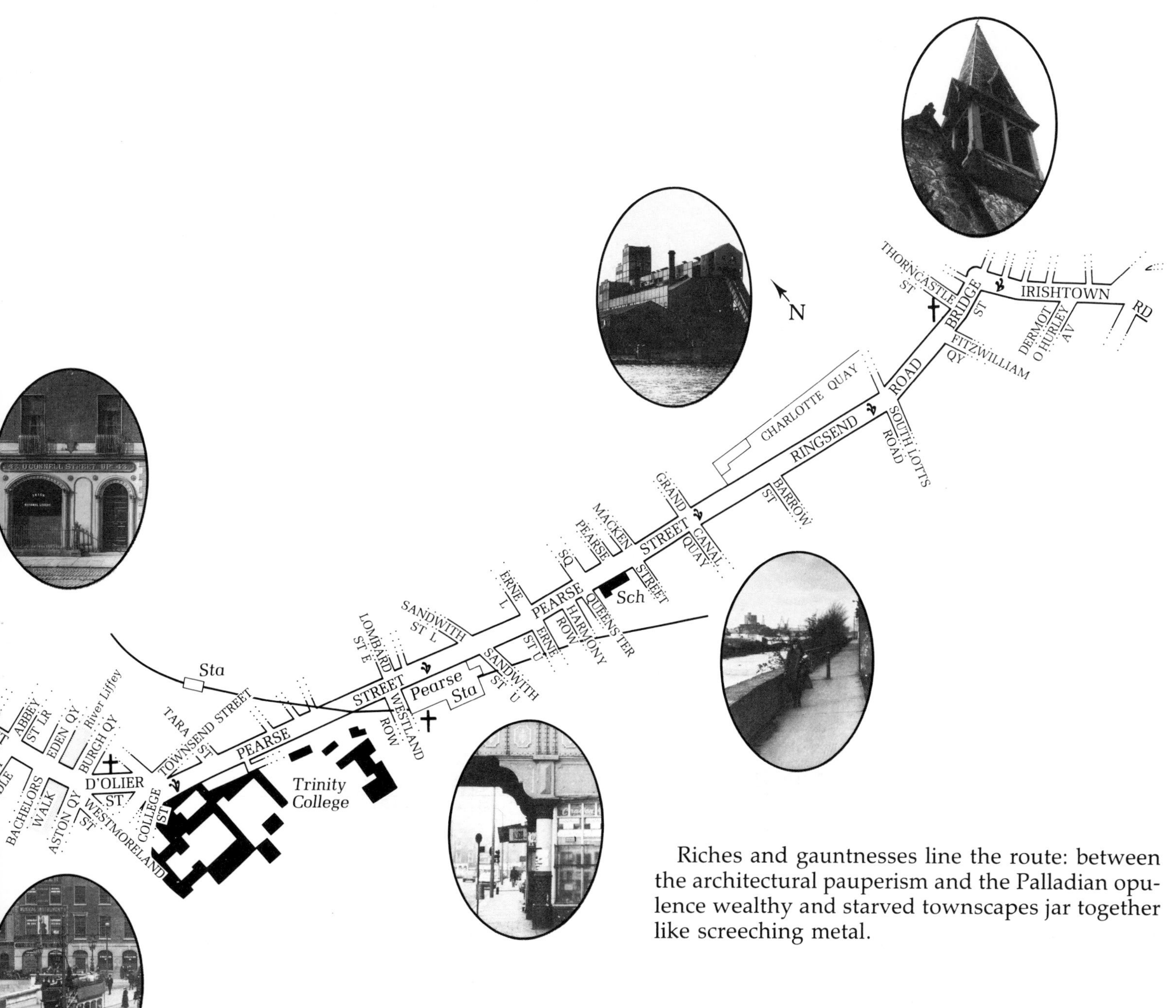

Riches and gauntnesses line the route: between the architectural pauperism and the Palladian opulence wealthy and starved townscapes jar together like screeching metal.

Stately, sombre, stepping slow
The white-plumed funeral horses go
With coaches crawling in their wake
A long and slow black glittering snake.
Inside of every crawling yoke
Silent cronies sit and smoke . . .

(This poet, Seumas O'Sullivan, had an eve-of-departure letter from Joyce: "1 toothbrush and powder. 1 nail brush. 1 pair of black boots and any coat and vest you have to spare.")

The General Post Office porticoed by, where a nation without a placenta was born in 1916 and to whose fame generations of patriots laid subsequent claim – the building simply isn't big enough to house everybody who pint-insists he was there on Easter Monday. Atop, Hibernia, Mercury, Fidelity: inside, the mythical warrior Cuchulainn, the Hound of Ulster, undead to his enemies until a raven pranced on his shoulder. Trollope was an official of the Post Office; up the street, Percy Bysshe Shelley threw pamphlets from his window encouraging the Irish to cast off the yoke. In 1966 they blew up the last vestiges of imperial Sackville Street by toppling Nelson and his pillar in the small furtive hours – plastic explosives marked fifty years of freedom, independence and maturity.

"Dead side of the street this. Dull business by day, land agents, temperance hotel, Falconer's railway guide, civil service college, Gill's, catholic club, the industrious blind." Hasn't changed much since Mr. Bloom's mental procession, fast food, an airline, a cinema sit suitable side by side, "under the patronage of Father Mathew", the apostle who laid temperance with a capital T on the Irish nation of drinkers in the mid-nineteenth century. "Ah, Father Mathew. A decent man – but a bit narrow-minded," declared a thirsty Abbey play, and every year in front of his Tipperary home the daffodils grow "T.M.", Theobald Mathew.

"White horses with white frontlet plumes came round the Rotunda corner, galloping. A tiny coffin flashed by. In a hurry to bury. A mourning coach. Unmarried. Black for the married. Piebald for bachelors. Dun for a nun."

There were thatched cottages once where the Rotunda is now, the first maternity hospital. The Assembly Rooms, by the lying-in hospital, became by Joycean juxtaposition the Gate Theatre. Up Rutland Square, indexed by the high frosted cornices of Findlater's Church, all one-way now. Is it a Joycean joke, or an affirmation of life, that one-way Dublin runs from, not *to*, Glasnevin cemetery? "The carriage climbed more slowly the hill of Rutland Square. Rattle his bones. Over the stones. Only a pauper. Nobody owns." Round the corner from Rutland Square Joyce was a pupil at Belvedere College. His academic skills brought the family spasms of prosperity, improvident trips to Jammet's Restaurant. His father asked once what gift Jim wanted if he won a forthcoming prize. "Two chops."

Up the hill, Blessington Street, Berkeley Street, Berkeley Road.

> The carriage galloped round a corner: stopped.
>
> What's wrong now?
>
> A divided drove of branded cattle passed the windows, lowing, slouching by on padded hoofs, whisking their tails slowly on their clotted bony croups. Outside them and through them ran raddled sheep bleating their fear.
>
> Emigrants, Mr. Power said.

For the boat certainly, down from the iron-clad acres of the cattle market, of the squared, hutted, fenced cobbleyards, came the browned, heaving, glinting, streaming kine, lurching to death.

Past the other end of Eccles Street. "My house down there." Molly, gleaming by now in the

TYLERS BOOTS
ROTUNDA. DUBLIN. 6427. W.L.

morning. Left into North Circular Road, up the slope. "Dunphy's Corner. Mourning coaches drawn up drowning their grief. A pause by the wayside. Tiptop position for a pub. Expect we'll pull up here on the way back to drink his health. Pass round the consolation. Elixir of life." Turned right again down Phibsborough Road over Cross Guns Bridge, past the Brian Boru pub, left into Prospect Road. On the right, at the bridge, the towers of Mountjoy Jail: on the left the Royal Canal sidles sluggishly into the bright fields of Kildare.

The carriage steered left for Finglas Road.

The stonecutter's yard on the right. Last lap. Crowded on the spit of land silent shapes appeared, white, sorrowful, holding out calm hands, knelt in grief, pointing. Fragments of shapes, hewn. In white silence: appealing. The best obtainable. Thos. H. Dennany, monumental builder and sculptor.

Glasnevin at last, poplar trees, groves of graves, little avenues of silence, O'Connell, Parnell, the towering dead.

Joyce believed that the word *Odysseus* came from *Outis* and *Zeus* – "nobody" and "god". Outiszeus-Ulysses-Bloom went down to the place of graves. The gods had warned Ulysses that in order to enter Hades safely he had to cut a trench in the ground a cubit long and a cubit broad. On the walls around Glasnevin are nineteenth century watchtowers erected to spotlight body-snatchers, often led by that knave of spades, the Sexton.

"White shapes thronged amid the trees, white forms and fragments streaming by mutely sustaining vain gestures on the air." In Hades Ulysses met the shades of the great and grateful dead. In Glasnevin Mr. Bloom eyed his way past the O'Connell circle, outward by Parnell's harped grave, thinking of rot and worm and shroud and

corpse. When John Joyce died Jim sent a friend out into the street to give money in commemoration to any indigent old man. And he wrote a poem: "O Father forsaken Forgive your son." In a letter to T. S. Eliot: "He had an intense love for me and it adds anew to my grief and remorse that I did not go to Dublin to see him for so many years." "Hades" is the chapter of the heart; "a man's inmost heart": "through the heart"; "hearts of grace", as many as twenty hearts in the chapter.

Poor Dignam is in the ground, noon approaches. "Mr. Bloom walked unheeded along his grove by saddened angels, crosses, broken pillars, family vaults, stone hopes praying with upcast eyes, old Ireland's hearts and hands."

AEOLUS

In the middle of the city Mr. Bloom comes to take his noontide place.

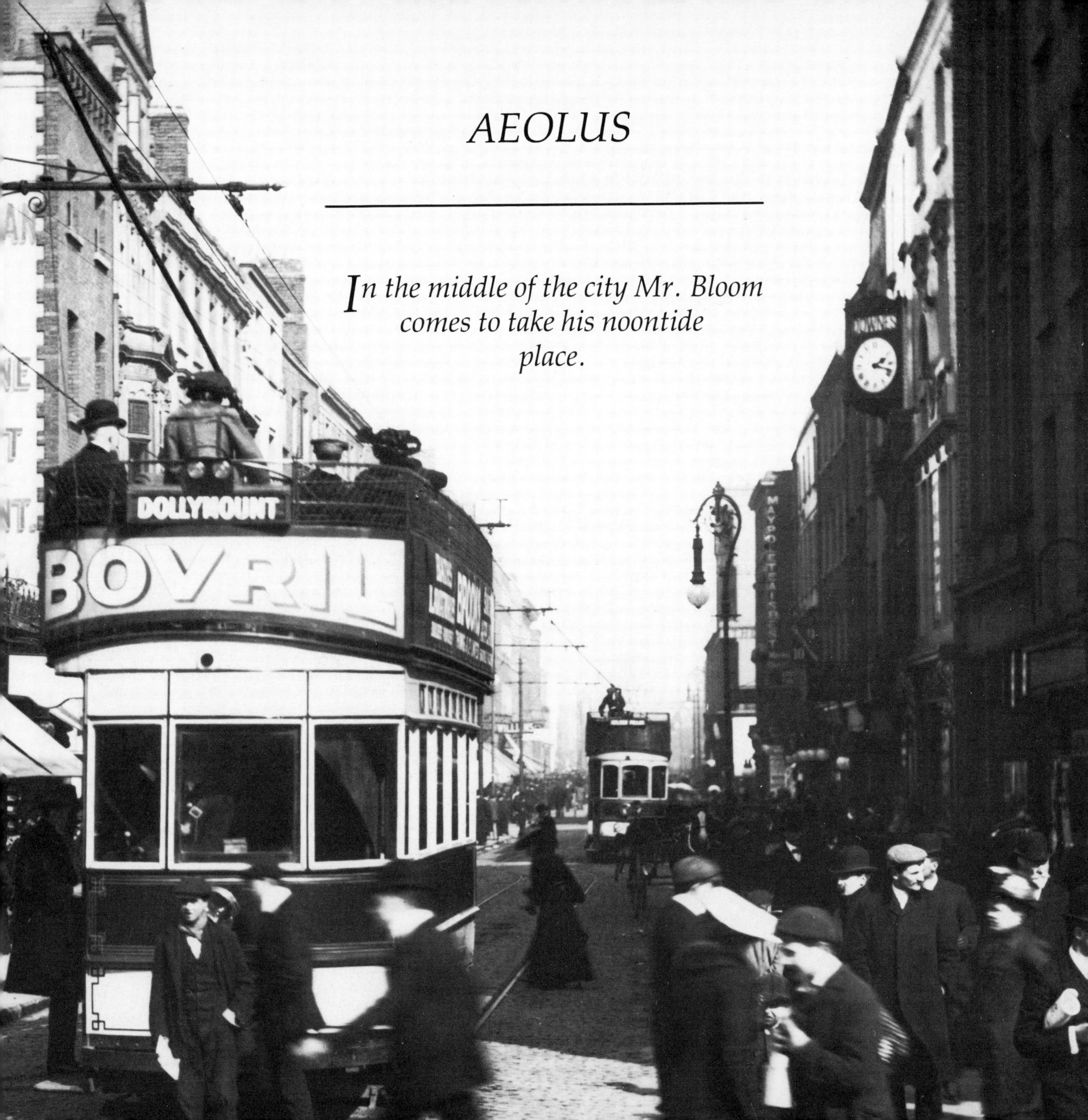

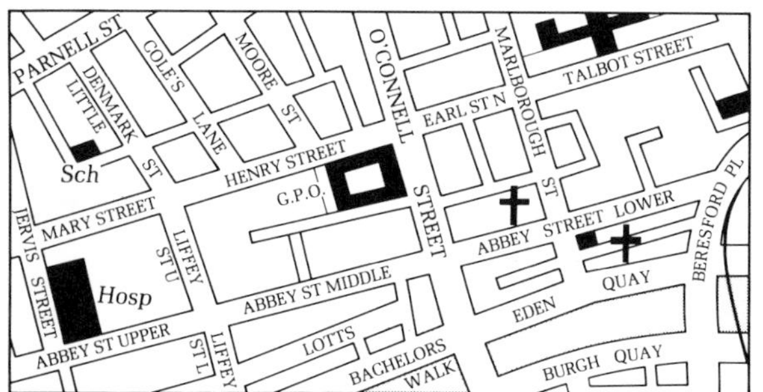

Mr. Leopold Bloom is a canvasser for newspaper advertisements, paid by results, a purchaser of time and space. When Ulysses arrived at the cave of Aeolus, the guardian of the breezes, that inventor of sail gave him a wine-skin full of propitious winds to speed him home. Mr. Bloom has arrived at the offices of the *Freeman's Journal* where he intends to transact business. In "Aeolus" Mr. Joyce gives the first hint that perhaps not everybody is endeared to Mr. Bloom.

The *Freeman's Journal* eventually, after a burning and a breaking of its presses by I.R.A. Civil Warriors, merged with Parnell's newspaper, the *Irish Independent,* whose main entrance is on Middle Abbey Street. Princes Street and O'Connell Street complete a wedge of buildings from which flow several newspapers. Joyce used the lungs as the symbol, the organic motto of the "Aeolus" chapter; news is inhaled, dwelt upon, and exhaled gustily, gaseously.

James Joyce's career as a writer began in University debates on his new passion, Ibsen. "I have read, or rather, spelt out", wrote Ibsen to an intermediary "a review by Mr. James Joyce in the *Fortnightly Review* which is very benevolent and for which I should greatly like to thank the author if only I had sufficient knowledge of the language." Joyce replied that he was a mere eighteen-year-old Irishman, that he would keep the words of Ibsen in his heart all his life, – and spent the twelve-guinea fee in glee and haste. Richard Ellman in his biography comments that Joyce had entered the world of literature "under the best auspices". With such Parnassian encouragement, he read voraciously, learned, enquired, rampaged through the minds of authors,novelists, playwrights, poets and essayists. Even language was no barrier: his headlong propulsion into literature culminated in a fulsome, flowing letter to Ibsen where despite "highest excellence" and "lofty impersonal power", he decreed that he, Joyce, was no hero-worshipper: but he had nonetheless deliberately acquired Dano-Norwegian, in order to write to Ibsen.

EVENING
PRESS
for small ads

GENTLEMEN OF THE PRESS

Grossbooted draymen rolled barrels dullthudding out of Prince's stores and bumped them up on the brewery float. On the brewery float bumped dullthudding barrels rolled by grossbooted draymen out of Prince's stores.

There it is, Red Murray said. Alexander Keyes.

Just cut it out, will you? Mr Bloom said, and I'll take it round to the *Telegraph* office.

Mr. Bloom is in the offices of the *Freeman's Journal* where he is reviving an advertisement for a purveyor of tea, wine and spirits. His client, Alexander Keyes, wants something special, two keys crossed at the top of his advertisement, already used successfully in a Kilkenny newspaper. Mr. Keyes' enterprise will be puffed editorially, provided the merchant takes three months of advertising in the newspaper. Mr. Bloom agrees to solicit time in return for space.

A DAYFATHER

He walked on through the caseroom, passing an old man, bowed, spectacled, aproned. Old Monks, the dayfather. Queer lot of stuff he must have put through his hands in his time: obituary notices, pubs' ads, speeches, divorce suits, found drowned.

Joyce wrote the "Aeolus" chapter in a parody of the newspaperman's style, headlines blowing forth from the Cave of the Winds.

AND IT WAS THE FEAST OF THE PASSOVER

He stayed in his walk to watch a typesetter neatly distributing type. Reads it backwards

first. Quickly he does it. Must require some practice that. mangiD. kcirtaP. Poor Papa with his hagadah book, reading backwards with his finger to me.

James Joyce's father, redundant from his official position, took an occasional job as an advertisement canvasser for the *Freeman's Journal.* James Joyce himself wrote several reports and reviews. His career with one newspaper ended so acrimoniously that the editor finally threatened to kick him down the stairs.

SPOT THE WINNER

Lenehan came out of the inner office with *Sports* tissues.

Who wants a dead cert for the Gold Cup? he asked. Sceptre with O. Madden up.

He tossed the tissues on to the table.

Screams of newsboys barefoot in the hall rushed near and the door was flung open.

Hush, Lenehan said. I hear footsteps.

Professor MacHugh strode across the room and seized the cringing urchin by the collar as the others scampered out of the hall and down the steps.

Mr. Bloom is hurrying back and forth, buffeted by the winds of advertising and editorial: he leaves the newspaper offices to find his client in a nearby auction room. There follows mocking his mazurka walk, "a file of capering newsboys in Mr. Bloom's wake, the last zigzagging white on the breeze a mocking kite, a tail of white bowknots".

Bachelor's Walk, where Bloom is headed, runs at right angles to O'Connell Street. Mr. Bloom's view, had he cared to stop, was of ships and seafarers, of bonneted ladies and bucks, of trams and tramp steamers: and for the second time that day he has missed Stephen Dedalus, who has arrived to deliver Mr. Deasy's letter.

Today, on Bachelor's Walk, the same small auction rooms (frequented by Alexander Keyes, purveyor of tea, wine and spirits, where he is discovered by Mr. Bloom): brass, the wood of ages, carpets, gathered in, and exhaled with the auctioneer's ten per cent added. Outside Mr. Bloom accosts the pubward editor, Myles Crawford.

House of keys, don't you see? His name is Keyes. It's a play on the name. But he practically promised he'd give the renewal. But he wants just a little puff. What will I tell him, Mr. Crawford?

K.M.A.

Will you tell him he can kiss by arse? Myles Crawford said, throwing out his arm for emphasis. Tell him that straight from the stable.

And Mr. Bloom, excluded, stands diplomatically on the street, watches the receding back of young Dedalus, "the moving spirit. Has a good pair of boots on him today. Last time I saw him he had his heels on view. Been walking in muck somewhere. Careless chap. What was he doing in Irishtown?" The tram which went from Glasnevin to Rialto bore a brown lozenge badge to indicate its route. From Nelson's pillar to Sandymount was indicated by a green crescent. A green shamrocked tram bore you to Dalkey, a green Maltese Cross from Rathfarnham to Drumcondra. Two blue diamonds decorated the tram which linked Donnybrook to the Phoenix Park and a white circle tram reached the quiet pools of Palmerston Park. It didn't, therefore, matter whether you could read. All that mattered was whether you walked. The tram conductor's

manual urged: "Keep a sharp lookout for passengers and by signalling, induce persons to travel who would otherwise walk."

A little phenomenon touched the tramways on Bloomsday – a little electrical phenomenon.

HELLO THERE, CENTRAL!

At various points along the eight lines tramcars with motionless trolleys stood in their tracks, bound for or from Rathmines, Rathfarnham, Blackrock, Kingstown and Dalkey, Sandymount Green, Ringsend and Sandymount Tower, Donnybrook, Palmerston Park and Upper Rathmines, all still, becalmed in short circuit.

G.P.O. & NELSON'S PILLAR. DUBLIN. 3496 W.L.

CADBURY'S
COCOA
KEHOE DONNELLY & PAKENHAM
LAWN MOWERS
139
LAWN MOWERS

LAESTRYGONIANS

From the square splay of O'Connell Bridge wide streets feel their way southward into an easier and richer city. The generous horizons forsake the common brick: elegant buildings ennoble Dublin with their cut stone.

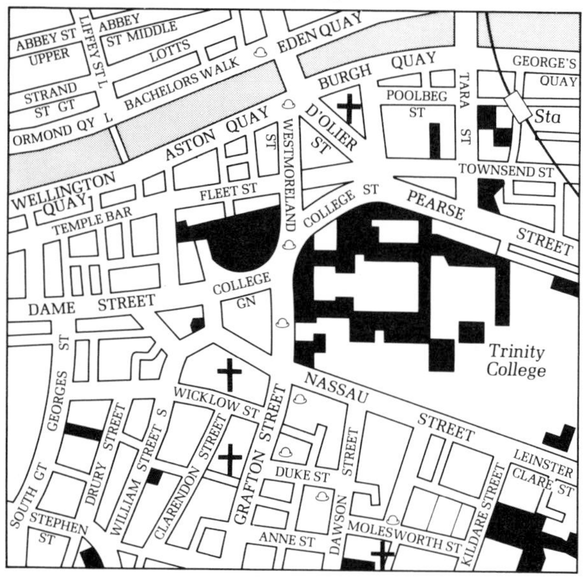

Think of O'Connell Street as the arm, O'Connell Bridge the hand: from the palm four fingers – Burgh Quay, D'Olier Street, Westmoreland Street, Aston Quay. The long finger is Westmoreland Street along which Mr. Bloom walked his pursed thoughtful way via College Green and Grafton Street; Duke Street means lunch: then over Dawson Street, to Molesworth Street, eventually faltering to a halt in Kildare Street. His journey begins at one o'clock, there is fitful sunshine, gently blown cloud.

"Pineapple rock, lemon platt, butter scotch. A sugar-sticky girl shovelling scoopfuls of cream for a christian brother." Mr. Bloom is thinking of food, of lunch, of Molly, of love. His destination is the National Library of Ireland in Kildare Street where he needs to make reference to that Kilkenny newspaper which has carried Mr. Keyes' advertisement with the keys crossed. "A sombre Y.M.C.A. young man, watchful among the warm sweet fumes of Graham Lemon's, placed a throwaway in a hand of Mr. Bloom." You will recall that Mr. Bloom has unwittingly tipped a horse called "Throwaway" (of whose existence he is unaware) for the Gold Cup. Now he is handed a throwaway piece of paper by a young evangelist: it suggests that Mr. Bloom be "washed in the blood of the lamb".

O'Connell Bridge was once Carlisle Bridge. "POPULACE APPLAUDS AS QUEEN VICTORIA PASSES OVER CARLISLE BRIDGE": but the *Irish Times* mischief-makers changed the "A" in "PASSES" to "I". Legend? How many bridges – and newspapers – claim the same tale? It took ten years to build Carlisle Bridge and its scaffolding was used as a gallows to hang renegade soldiers, with their coats turned inside out. "As he set foot on O'Connell Bridge a puffball of smoke plumed up from the parapet. Brewery barge with export stout." Dubliners, priorities in order, jest biblically about "the Book of Guinnesses". When Lord Moyne, brewery proprietor, was elevated to the House of Lords in London, one ancient blue-blooded peer, outraged at this ingress of trade, this mere brewer, queried querulously: "Who is this fellow Moyne, anyway?" The new noble Lord was jubil-

O'CONNELL BRIDGE, DUBLIN

ant: "Moyne's a Guinness." An Ulster poet Louis MacNeice coopered into shape the view from O'Connell Bridge:

. . . And the brewery tugs and the swans
On the balustraded stream
And the bare bones of a fanlight
Over a hungry door
And the air soft on the cheek
And porter running from the taps
With a head of yellow cream . . .

Flowers and lanterns light this broad bridge and political protestors pollute it with bearded shouts. "He threw down among them a crumpled paper ball." But Mr. Bloom's kind heart gets the better of him and he offers the kee-haaring gulls two crumbed Banbury cakes which he buys for a penny. Bread after the "blood of the lamb"? "Aware of their greed and cunning he shook the powdery crumb from his hands. They never expected that. Manna." Watch – Joyce is at it again. Mannanaan MacLir is the god of the waters and Mannanaan MacLir possesses magic pigs which though killed and eaten are re-generated every day. And, sure enough, a few lines later: "eat pig like pig". Manna, Mannanaan MacLir. Pig like pig. O, Joyce!

"Timeball on the ballast office is down." It is one o'clock, Mr. Bloom is thinking of food and Molly's sharp wit. "She used to say Ben Dollard had a base barreltone voice. He had legs like barrels and you'd think he was singing into a barrel." The ballast office is no more, and this corner of Westmoreland Street and Aston Quay is housed anew. Mr. Bloom stood and watched a procession of whitesmocked sandwich boards. "He read the scarlet letters on their five tall white hats: H.E.L.Y.S. Wisdom Hely's. Y lagging behind drew a chunk of bread from under his foreboard, crammed into his mouth and munched as he walked.

Mr. Bloom crosses Westmoreland Street "when apostrophe S had plodded by." Thinking still about Molly and food and Molly and rabbit pie, "he walked along the curbstone. Stream of life." Mr. Bloom loves his wife.

O, Mr. Bloom, how do you do?
O, how do you do, Mrs. Breen?
No use complaining. How is Molly those times? Haven't seen her for ages.
In the pink, Mr. Bloom said gaily, Milly has a position down in Mullingar, you know.

A typical Dublin greeting, it even has a tune.

How is your oul' wan? Game Ball.
Who was she out with? Meehawl.
What did she give him? Damn-all.

Mr. Bloom tells of the death of poor Dignam. "Sad to lose the old friends, Mrs. Breen's womaneyes said melancholily." Mrs. Breen's daft husband is a great one for the litigation. "He's a caution to rattlesnakes." Mr. Bloom's tastebuds begin to blossom, to bloom even, in his nostrils "hot mockturtle vapour and steam of newbaked jampuffs rolypoly". Mrs. Breen's husband is difficult – the new moon.

Mr. Bloom said:

Mind! Let this man pass.

A bony form strode along the curbstone from the river, staring with a rapt gaze into the sunlight through a heavy stringed glass. Tight as a skullpiece a tiny hat gripped his head. From his arm a folded dustcoat, a stick and an umbrella dangled to his stride.

AND AT
INTMENT.

> Watch him, Mr. Bloom said. He always walks outside the lampposts. Watch!

Cashel Boyle O'Connor Fitzmaurice Tisdall Farrell always walked at great speed *outside* the lampposts.

Bang-bang from Inchicore brandished, gun-like, a large key, yelling, "Bang. Bang. You're dead". Zozimus, the blind ballad-maker, wandered in the walled shadows of the Old City making songs for the children. The Bird Flanagan bought and paid for a Christmas turkey hanging outdoors in Nassau Street. Telling the shopkeeper he would collect it later, he hung about until he saw two patrolling policemen. Then he charged along the pavement, grabbed the bird from its hook and ran, luring the policemen into a full hue and cry. Endymion Farrell was the son of a brewer. He fell into a vat and never recovered his equilibrium: he carried a sword and a fishing rod and his little bowler hat had large holes in it for ventilation.

Cashel Boyle O'Connor Fitzmaurice Tisdall Farrell recurs in *Ulysses,* a rushing breeze along the pavements.

Mr. Bloom moves on, Mrs. Breen moves off.

> Same blue dress she had two years ago, the nap bleaching. Seen its best days. Wispish hair over her ears. And that dowdy toque, three old grapes to take the harm out of it. Shabby genteel. She used to be a tasty dresser. Lines round her mouth. Only a year or so older than Molly.

Mr. Bloom passed the *Irish Times,* since moved round the corner. In it he had placed the advertisement which found Martha: "Wanted lady typist to aid gentleman in literary work." Mr. Bloom reflects on the *Irish Times'* small ads, its news of earls and clergy, thoughts of ladies astride horses, the woman climbing on the sidecar outside the Gros-

DUFF

venor Hotel that morning, Lady Mountcashel with the Ward Union Staghounds "riding astride", daring. A Tipperary huntress, Mrs. Delaney, galloped to hounds blowing a hunting horn and smoking a cigarette simultaneously. And when challenged with the cruel knowledge that her poor horse was sweating distressedly, said between hunting horn and cigarette: "Little man, if you'd been between my legs for the past five hours you'd be sweating too."

When James Joyce met Nora Barnacle for the first time (on the 10th of June 1904) she thought he was a sailor. He wore a yachting cap, had deep blue eyes. Swedish? She was a chambermaid in Finn's Hotel on South Leinster Street, tall, strong and striking and he addressed her, serendipitily, on Nassau Street. She came from Galway and when Joyce's father heard her name, "Barnacle", he is said to have exclaimed: "Jaysus, I suppose she'll stick to him anyway." They made an appointment to meet, on the 14th, outside the Wildes of Merrion Square. Nora jilted, but a letter later she agreed to meet again, and on the 16th of June they went walking. She was a straightforward, simple country girl who satisfied Joyce's need for the ordinary – but could be tart and brusque when stirred. Joyce loved her as Mr. Bloom loves Molly, thought of her constantly, laughed at her wit, addressed his letters: "Dear Little Brown Head". She had elementary education, at thirteen was a menial employee, rarely read, never her husband's work, but defended him vigorously, even when a priest asked her during Confession to try and stop her husband writing "those terrible books". In later life Nora observed: "I *don't* know whether he's a genius, but I *do* know there's nobody like him." Joyce's Ulysses also thinks endlessly about his Molly, a sensuous debt on his soul, a watermark.

"He crossed under Tommy Moore's roguish finger." Moore was a social climber with courtly ambitions and despite his sweet, sweet, song-making Dublin turned against him. "They did right to put him up over a urinal: meeting of the waters." Old Dublin joke. Moore's melody went: "There is not in this wide world a valley so sweet/ As that vale in whose bosom the bright waters meet." The lavatory attendant under Moore's statue, questioned on the unsavoury raw materials, the commodities he dealt with every day, protested: "Sure, isn't it my bread and butter."

"His smile faded as he walked, a heavy cloud hiding the sun slowly, shadowing Trinity's surly front." This is College Green: before the light of learning filtered through its railings and pillars it was an archery green, and Mystery Plays were performed. Trinity College was created in 1592, blessed from afar by Queen Elizabeth I: founded on the site of a priory whose tower was a navigation aid to sailors in the bay: developed as a "breeding-ground for Protestants and patriots". Once it was an excommunicable act for a Catholic to attend Trinity – now the majority rules. On the lawn, rented from the Dublin Corporation in exchange for a chicken towards the Lord Mayor's pot, stand statues of Edmund Burke and Oliver Goldsmith, politician and poet. They shared a sculptor, their legs are identical. Impoverished Goldsmith attended Trinity as a sizar, a position obtainable elsewhere only in Cambridge – the College paid his fees, he paid in pride. He served the Fellows, cleaned the Squares, wore a humiliatingly obvious red cap. In London later, in the company of Dr. Johnson and Sir Joshua Reynolds, he gained subtle, social revenge by assuring Society that whereas they chewed with the lower jaw he alone chewed with the upper!

Across College Green the twenty-two pillars of the Bank of Ireland support statues of, left to right, Commerce, Hibernia, Fidelity. A bank since 1789,

NESTLES
MILK
Reckitts Blue
ZEBRA
GRATE POLISH
188

it once Housed the Parliament – and official Irish Bulls: "Why should we do anything for posterity," debated Boyle Roche, "what has posterity ever done for us?" Banking halls of high ceilings and old triumphal tapestries, brass and mahogany, long, whispering stone corridors, green lampshades and deep vaults, counting-houses, correspondence rooms, cobbled courtyards and a court of directors.

In the early 1960s I worked in this building, a slave to commercial splendour. Lunch was by ticket, promotion by age, survival by servility. Paternalism was pervasive, the right parlance and preoccupations – golf, hockey, tennis, rugby football, choir membership – important. Young men from mild commercial and professional families in country towns came to Dublin in new suits and stiff gaits to earn respect and a pension. Young women wore blue bodycoats and an air of passive distinction.

Much of the work was subterranean – in silvered neon Hadean vaults we counted coins from sacks into bags. The tedium was relieved by the wild Joycean language of the bucks whose recounted weekend exploits, no less entertaining for their apocryphy, whitewashed the ache until Wednesday when it was possible to look forward again.

The irreverence was endless. An elderly, haughty bank auditor was accustomed to wearing two pairs of trousers, the old protecting the striped. As he fumbled through his outside flies for his change inside, the bus conductor interpreted his action incorrectly and ejected him with angry prudery. Downstairs we laughed for a month.

J. R. R. Tolkien, a Visiting Examiner at Trinity, needed to cash a cheque, hadn't made the necessary advices, was refused upstairs in the banking hall. As he insisted on a confirmation by telephone to Trinity the reluctant clerk took down his name. "Tolkien," said the discomfited professor: "T-O-L-K-I-E-N. J.R.R.," wrote the clerk immediately and smiled up: "And how much money does the Lord of the Rings want today?" J. R. R. Tolkien always said Dublin was the most civilised city in Europe.

"Provost's House. The reverend Dr. Salmon: tinned salmon." Food again as Mr. Bloom treads past the most perfect house in Ireland, designed by Palladio himself. When Sir John Pentland Mahaffy, Oscar Wilde's tutor, was Provost of Trinity a cocktailed lady tweeted: "Dr. Mahaffy, you are a man, I a woman. In your learned opinion what, pray, is the essential difference between us?" "Madame, I can't conceive." Town and gown have merged since then.

Mr. Bloom sees the "haunting face" of John Howard Parnell, brother of Charles Stewart Parnell, the lost leader. Mr. Bloom is overtaken by two cyclists, George Russell of the famous pseudonym "A.E.", and Miss Lizzie Twigg, the literatus and his emanuensis. "His eyes followed the high figure in homespun, beard and bicycle, a listening woman at his side." Is this the same Lizzie Twigg who has replied to his advertisement in the *Irish Times*? "He crossed at Nassau Street corner and stood before the window of Yeates and Son, pricing the field glasses." Is it true that each side of Nassau Street is the sunny side?

"Grafton Street gay with housed awnings lured his senses. Muslin prints, silk, dames and dowagers, jingle of harnesses, hoofthuds lowringing in the baking causeway." The shopping area for the cream of Dublin – rich and thick. Very old Dublin joke. Coffee grinding in Bewleys' window, svelte mincing young women in fashion, Dublin on high heels. "He passed, dallying, the windows of Brown Thomas, silk mercers. Cascades of ribbons. Flimsy China silks. A tilted urn poured from its mouth a flood of bloodhued poplin: lustrous blood." The sun has come out again and Mr. Bloom's hunger drives him to seek a collation, but the diners in the Burton Restaurant on Duke Street are repellent. "Perched on high stools by the bar, hats shoved back, at the tables calling for more bread no charge, swilling, wolfing gobfuls of sloppy food, their eyes bulging, wiping wetted moustaches. A pallid suetfaced young man polished his tumbler knife fork and spoon with his napkin." Poor Mr. Bloom. "A man with an infant's saucestained napkin tucked around him shovelled gurgling soup down his gullet. A man spitting back on his plate: halfmasticated gristle: no teeth to chewchewchew it." Mr. Bloom made an excuse and left, went along the street to Davy Byrne's. In Duke Street now, the Bailey Restuarant enlightenedly houses the door of Number Seven Eccles Street. Across in Davy Byrne's Mr Bloom takes a glass of Burgundy and a sandwich. Watch! Again! "Sandwich? Ham and his descendants mustered and bred there." Bloom the Jew. Ham. Mustard. Bread. Grrr! Joyce!

It was not unusual for James Joyce to be hungry.

Telefón
LUAN-AOINE
16.00 18.30
MON-FRI

Richard Ellmann recounts a meeting between Joyce and Gogarty.

> Gogarty asked: "Where have you been for two days, Were you ill?" "Yes." "What were you suffering from?" "Inanition," Joyce answered without hesitation. His hunger fed his pride.

In Paris he cadged meals, in Trieste the Joyces frequently went without. On his visit home to Dublin in 1909 relatives remarked on how thin he had become. And in London in the Thirties he cooled for ever to a friend who took him to an indifferent restaurant.

Joyce wrote the "Laestrygonians" episode of *Ulysses* as a peristaltic parallel to the human digestive system: food is the dominant commodity, streetside sweetstalls, cakes cast upon the waters, Dr. Salmon, John Howard Parnell has "poached eyes on ghost" in his haunting face, Mrs. Breen was a "tasty dresser". When Ulysses finally left Aeolus and the Cave of the Winds he and his crew sailed for six days and six nights and on the seventh day reached Laestrygonia. There, his scouts were devoured and his ships attacked by the giant Laestrygonian cannibals who speared men like fish and ate them raw. Ulysses Bloom escaped too, from the ogred foulness of the Burton Restaurant to the calm of Davy Byrnes.

"Mr. Bloom ate his strips of sandwich, fresh clean bread, with relish of disgust, pungent mustard, the feety savour of green cheese." Not ham, of course, gorgonzola. "Glowing wine on his palate lingered swallowed." A memory is touched, of Molly lying on Howth Head, in fern beneath him, kissing, yielding, wild. As Mr. Bloom goes out to the yard Nosey Flynn and Davy Byrne discuss him. Paddy Leonard, Bantam Lyons and Tom Rochford enter and discuss the Gold Cup. "Mr. Bloom on his way out raised three fingers in greeting." Nobody yet believes Bantam Lyons that he received a tip for "Throwaway" from the prudent Jew.

"Mr. Bloom walked towards Dawson Street, his tongue brushing his teeth smooth." It is almost two o'clock and he helps a blind youth across Dawson Street into Molesworth Street. Up ahead, Leinster House is a broad forehead, to the left the Masonic Headquarters. Molesworth Street has fared better than some: the new architecture is not entirely without character. Mr. Bloom sees yet again "straw hat in sunlight. Tan shoes. Turnedup trousers. It is. It is." Blazes Boylan, the organiser of Molly Bloom. Agitated, wrinkled with cuckoldry, Mr. Bloom flees with the wine on his face. As if he were referring to papers in his pocket he flutters off-course to the Museum instead of the nearby Library. "Yes. Gate. Safe!."

SCYLLA AND CHARYBDIS

The National Library of Ireland is a rounded fort, a columned temple. Like twin stone urns, the Library and the Museum stand in the yard of Government, storing the essence of the nation.

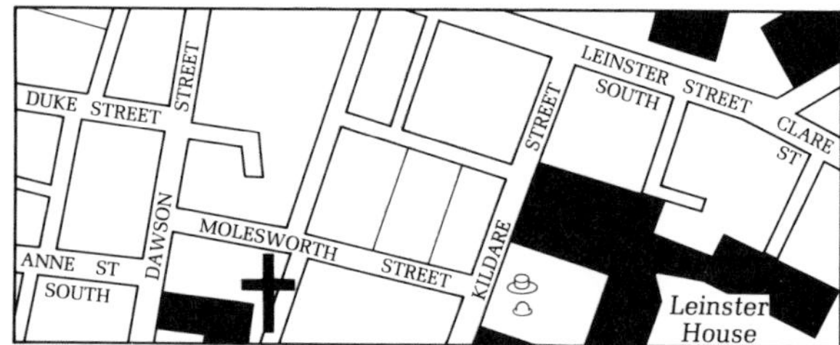

Uncurved Kildare Street is quiet and wide from St. Stephen's Green in the south to College Park wall on Nassau Street to the north. Trees dress each end. Nubian princesses and their slaves light the entrance to the Shelbourne Hotel on the Green corner, monkeys and birds are chased into the wall of the old Kildare Street Club on the Nassau Street corner. This is an official street, dominated by Dail Eireann, the Irish Lower House and Senate. Government offices stand civilly by, a few happy little shops wink from behind the official skirts.

When Joyce left the Martello Tower in Sandycove in a frightened huff, he walked the nine miles to the National Library to expand a theory. Stephen Dedalus, since quaffing with newspapermen, makes his way to the National Library to discourse upon acquaintances. The first is "Bald, most zealous" Lyster, the Quaker librarian. Then, "Mr. Best entered, tall, young, mild, light" and destined to be Lyster's successor, refuser of small loans to J. Joyce, Esq.

W. K. Magee, also on the Library staff, used the nom-de-plume "John Eglinton", was nicknamed "Stiff-breeches" by Joyce; a careful man, elegant essayist, he eschewed drink, women, wild imaginings and was, therefore, in Joyce's ink, a butt:

There once was a Celtic librarian
Whose essays were voted Spencerian
His name is Magee
But it seems that to me
He's a flavour that's more Presbyterian.

The fourth of Stephen's energetic listeners is George Russell, Mr. Bloom's high, tweedy cyclist. As "A.E.", Russell was Dublin's principal literary host. Joyce, at twenty, ambitiously anticipatory, wanted his name scribbled in Russell's address book and called on him unannounced one chiming midnight, and used two hours to damn all Russell's literary ilk by comparison with the Artist as a young man. Kind, mystic and bearded, Russell thought Joyce the wildest young man he had ever known:

"Proud as Lucifer and writes verses perfect in their technique and sometimes beautiful in quality." It worked. Russell spoke in his circle, a new cup-and-saucer was put on the tray for tea. But he told the youth to acquire more chaos.

> "What is a ghost? Stephen said with tingling energy. One who has faded into impalpability through death, through absence, through change of manners. Elizabethan London lay as far from Stratford as corrupt Paris lies from virgin Dublin. Who is the ghost from *limbo patrum,* returning to the world that has forgotten him? Who is King Hamlet?

Even as Joyce dwelt in the Tower at Sandycove he had begun to work out his theory that Shakespeare was Hamlet's father, the dead King whom Will loved to play. That Hamlet was the young Hamnet Shakespeare,Will's only son who died at the age of twelve. That while Shakespeare was in London Ann Hathaway enjoyed Will's brothers, a betraying Queen. Leopold Bloom is a cuckold with a dead son.

34

The Reading Room of the National Library of Ireland, Kildare Street, Dublin, 2, is a fertile, peaceful acre. Curvilinear, styled like the Parliament in Oslo, built in 1890 by Sir Thomas Deane and Sir Thomas Deane – Deane and Son – it houses the photographs in the Lawrence Collection, the stiffened ghosts of ribboned ladies, hatted gentlemen and harnessed animals recorded on glass, preserved on microfilm. Of the thousand copies printed in the Shakespeare and Co. first edition of *Ulysses*, published by Sylvia Beach in Paris in 1922, the National Library contains volume number 999 and volume number one. Rich wood, green shades, old files of newspapers with the names of mythical citizens: *The Kerryman, The Clare Champion, The Dundalk Argus, The Cork Examiner, The Anglo-Celt, The Munster Tribune, The Nationalist,* printed provincial demigods awaiting consultation.

Joyce believed that the brain was busiest and best in the afternoon. The episode in the National Library represents the brain. Scylla and Charybdis, to complicate matters, are the twin cliffs of Platonic and Aristotleian thought between which Stephen is trying to steer, without being sucked into the eddy of confusion. "Ineffable", "Supreme", "deepest", "heavenly", "beautiful" are globes which glow in Stephen's illumination of the Bard.

Shakespeare was one of Joyce's few gods. Stephen is about to insist that Shakespeare's well-known inferiority complex was due to Ann Hathaway's seducing him, stealing the sexual initiative, when: "Amen! responded from the doorway." And "with a ribald face, sullen as a dean's, Buck Mulligan came forwards then blithe in motley, towards the greeting of their smiles". The mocker is back, double-dactyl Malachi Mulligan.

Stephen hadn't kept their tavern appointment, ("The Ship, Buck Mulligan cried. Half twelve" – remember?) and telegraphed his absence to the exaggeratedly aggrieved Buck. "And we to be there, mavrone, and you to be unbeknownst sending us your conglomerations the way we to have our tongues out a yard long like the drouthy clerics do be fainting for a pussful." It was a Golden Age in Dublin. Synge, Gogarty, Shaw, Russell, Moore, Colum, O'Sullivan, O'Casey – foothills on whom the lava flowed from the high fiery cones of Yeats and Joyce. "Mr. Lyster, an attendant said from the door ajar." Enter Mr. Bloom. "There's a gentleman here, sir, the attendant said, coming forward and offering a card. From the *Freeman*. He wants to see the files of the *Kilkenny People* for last year." Mulligan has just seen Mr. Bloom by the statues in the museum, and Bloom knows Stephen's father, Simon. Shakespeare is resumed – much more lightly with mocking Mulligan. Stephen even tells the Shakespearean joke. Burbage, playing the Hunchback, arrived at the door of a lady fan. The Bard had intercepted the curtain call, and cried from the boudoir: "William the Conqueror came before Richard the Third." And Stephen is still brooding over his dead mother "hurrying to her squalid deathlain from gay Paris". Mother dying. Come home. Father.

"Every life is many days, day after day. We walk through ourselves, meeting robbers, ghosts, giants, old men, young men, wives, widows, brothers-in-love. But always meeting ourselves." Shakespeare ended, Stephen and the Buck Mulligan stand in the doorway "a man passed out between them, bowing, greeting". The Third Time. "The wandering Jew, Buck Mulligan whispered with clown's awe", mocking as the newsboys did, Mr. Bloom's departing back. Stephen still resents the Buck who chants airily of whores and mariners. Joyce softens. "Kind air defined the coigns of houses in Kildare Street. No birds. Frail from the housetops two plumes of smoke ascended, pluming, and in a flaw of softness softly were blown."

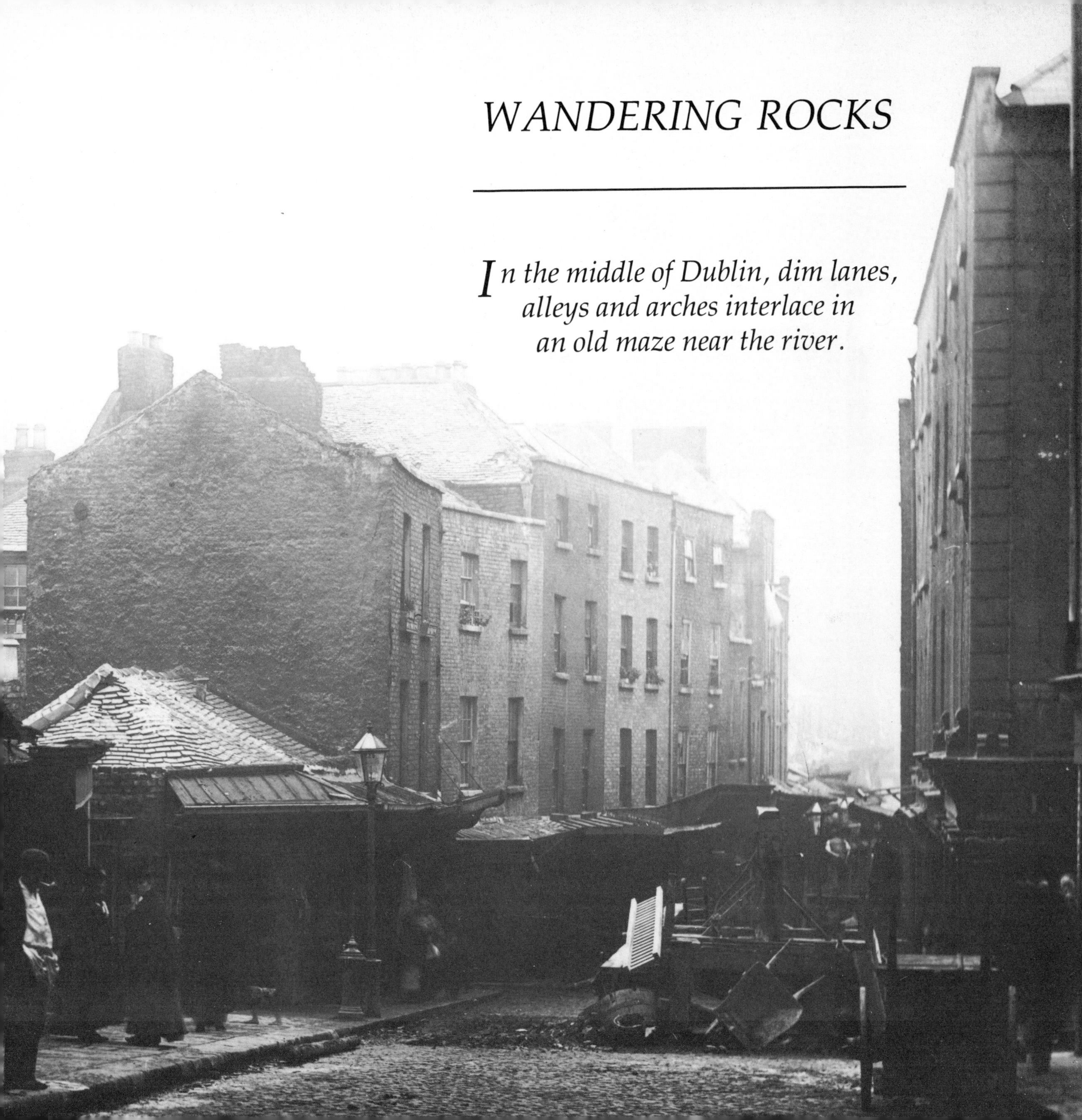

WANDERING ROCKS

In the middle of Dublin, dim lanes, alleys and arches interlace in an old maze near the river.

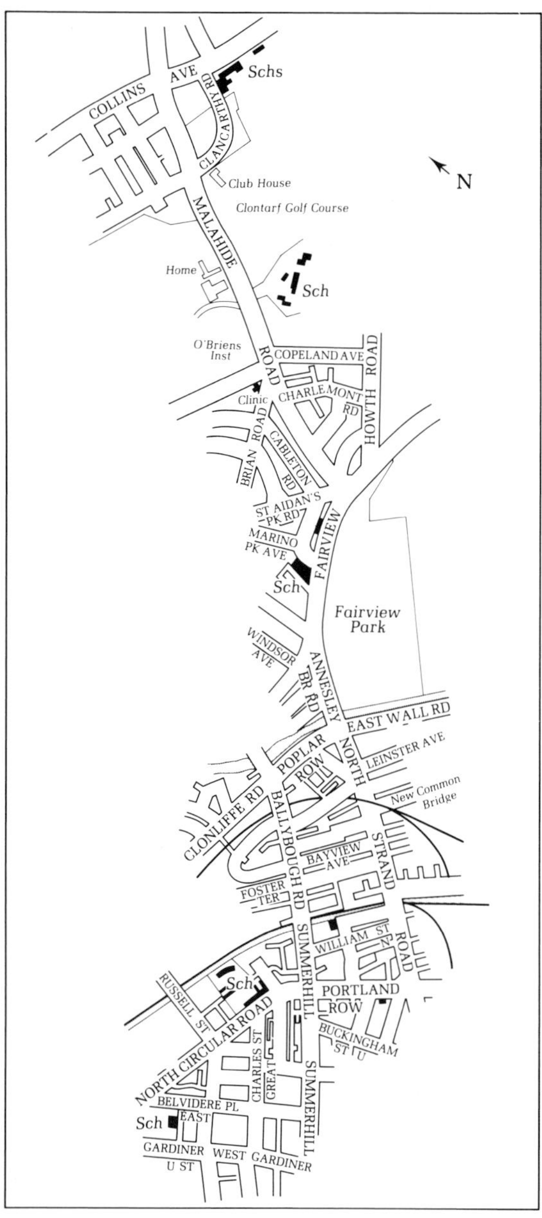

A broker of Space and Time, Joyce, while devising "Wandering Rocks", used compass, set-square, ruler and map – and a timepiece to arrange the movements of the characters in the episode; as a further aid he played every night a board game called "Labyrinth" with his daughter Lucia. In "Wandering Rocks", which comes halfway in the novel, neither Stephen Dedalus nor Leopold Bloom dominates. Here is the nub and core of Joycean Dublin; the "womancity" is the central character, hostess to her own people; her shores are mapped by her citizens on their un-epic voyages.

In his planning Joyce traced the two principal voyages in red ink – the first journey, made by a priest, the final one by the King's Governor-General. And between those parameters of Church and State a procession of the people of Dublin wander, walk, talk and wind their way about the business of the hour between three and four o'clock in the afternoon. Think of it as a busy Dutch painting, sixteenth or seventeenth century, Pieter Brueghel or Hendrik Avercamp – all those little figures dancing, skating, hunting, harvesting. In Dublin on the 16th of June, 1904, they are walking, talking, standing still.

Homer's heroes were advised to steer clear of the rocks which his blessed gods called the wanderers, past which it was fatal to sail, over which it was dangerous to fly. Joyce's people navigate their streams of consciousness with a similar weather eye to fortune and comedy, tragedy and mischance.

> The superior, the very Reverend John Conmee S.J., reset his smooth watch in his interior pocket as he came down the presbytery steps. Five to three. Just nice time to walk to Artane. What was that boy's name again? Dignam, yes. *Vere dignum et justum est.*

Father Conmee is on his way to the orphanage to see whether the son of the deceased Patrick Dignam may be admitted. A one-legged sailor held out a cap, and Father Conmee blessed him and crossed to Mountjoy Square, thinking of God and soldiers and sailors and cannonballs.

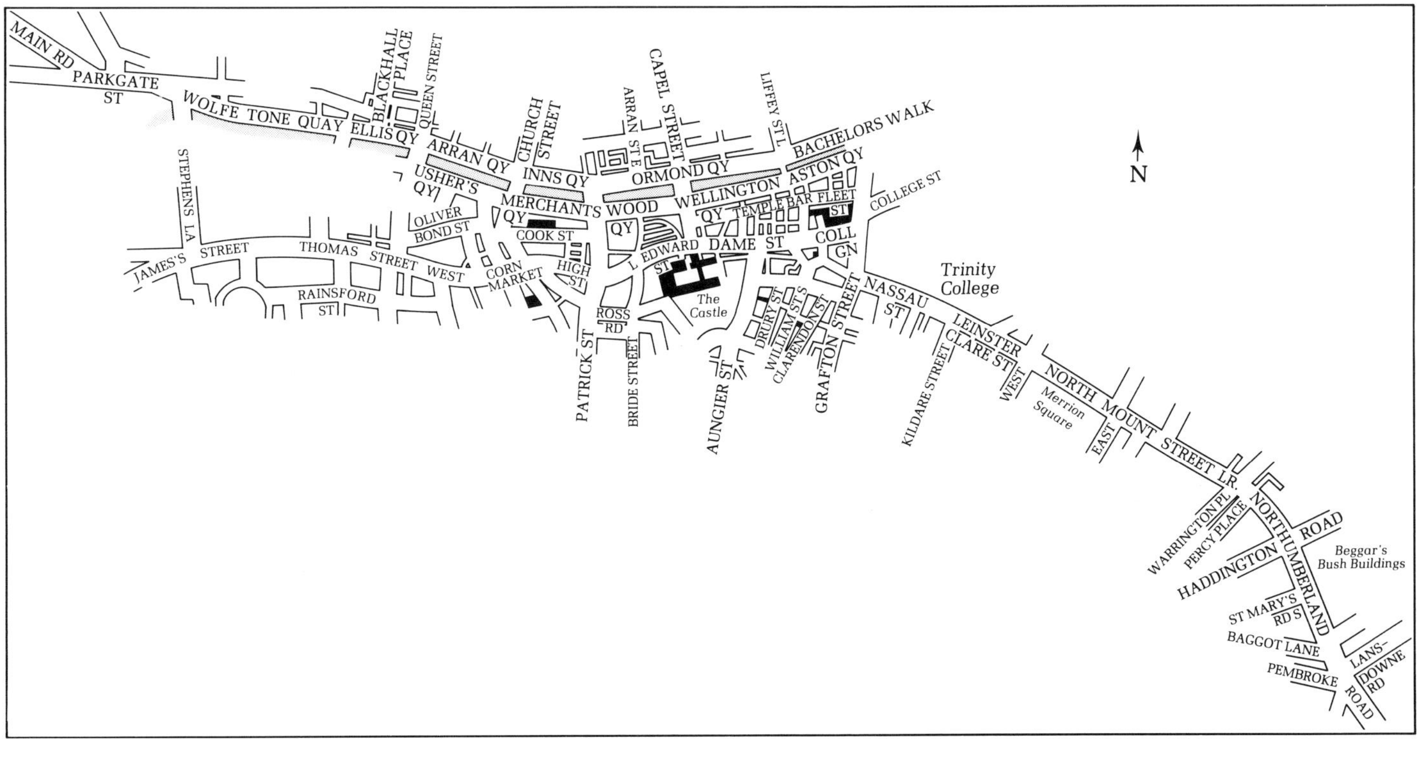

MAIN RD
PARKGATE ST
WOLFE TONE QUAY
ELLIS QY
BLACKHALL PLACE
QUEEN STREET
ARRAN QY
CHURCH STREET
INNS QY
ARRAN ST E
CAPEL STREET
ORMOND QY
LIFFEY ST
BACHELORS WALK
ASTON QY
WELLINGTON QY
USHER'S QY
MERCHANTS QY
WOOD QY
TEMPLE BAR
FLEET ST
COLLEGE ST
STEPHENS LA
OLIVER BOND ST
COOK ST
JAMES'S STREET
THOMAS STREET WEST
CORN MARKET
HIGH ST
EDWARD ST
DAME ST
COLL GN
RAINSFORD ST
ROSS RD
The Castle
NASSAU ST
Trinity College
LEINSTER
CLARE ST
PATRICK ST
BRIDE STREET
AUNGIER ST
DRURY ST
WILLIAM ST S
CLARENDON ST
GRAFTON STREET
KILDARE STREET
WEST
Merrion Square
EAST
NORTH MOUNT STREET LR.
N
WARRINGTON PL.
PERCY PLACE
NORTHUMBERLAND ROAD
HADDINGTON ROAD
Beggar's Bush Buildings
ST MARY'S RD S
BAGGOT LANE
PEMBROKE ROAD
LANS-DOWNE RD

Father Conmee was the Rector of Clongowes Wood, Joyce's first school. He was the Jesuit whom Joyce's dilapidated father met in Mountjoy Square one day and who immediately offered James a place in Belvedere College, nearby, where he had just become Prefect of Studies. To Joyce he was ever after "a bland and courtly humanist".

"Father Conmee walked down Great Charles Street and glanced at the shutup free church on his left", to the North Circular Road where there is "strangely no tramline", past the schools of Saint Joseph and by Aldborough House with its own theatre; it was the last genuine Palladian mansion to be built in Ireland. Father Conmee walked along the North Strand Road, smelling incense and baconflitches and butter, past Corny Kelleher, poor Dignam's undertaker, who "totted figures in the daybook while he chewed a blade of hay". Past

policemen and porkbutchers and bargemen and their horses on Newcomen Bridge, he "stepped on to an outward bound tram".

Bombs fell here in Hitler's war, neutral Eire's only wound. A limping German aircraft either jettisoned for speed, or got it all wrong, and the night came apart. This is no-man's-land, not city, not suburb, suitable only for travelling through and halting, as did Father Conmee's tram. By Annesley Bridge he descended and read his Latin breviary, hic-haec-hocking his way to Artane: into his path "a flushed young man came from a gap of the hedge and after him a young woman with wild nodding daisies in her hand". Father Conmee blessed them both "gravely and turned a thin page of his breviary". In "Wandering Rocks" only the representatives of Church and State move away from the city's heart.

"Mr. Dennis J. Maginni, professor of dancing, etc., in silk hat, slate frockcoat with silk facings, white kerchief tie, tight lavender trousers, canary gloves and pointed patent boots, walking with grave deportment . . ." Another of Dublin's characters on his way from his home in North Great Georges Street to the city centre. Is the dancing-master included to observe the element of time? With metronomic precision, the characters in "Wandering Rocks" walk only minutes away from each other. One-two, one-two-three-four. Tempo? Well, strict enough.

"Corny Kelleher sped a silent jet of hayjuice arching from his mouth while a generous white arm from a window in Eccles Street flung forth a coin", two glittering arcs simultaneously, miles apart. A one-legged sailor who earlier importuned Father John Conmee for alms, received instead a blessing, has pegged his way around the corner from Upper Gardiner Street into Dorset Street. As he turned into Eccles Street Molly Bloom flung the sailor a coin. "A plump bare generous arm shone, was seen, held forth from a white petticoatbodice and taut shiftstraps." All through "Wandering Rocks" Joyce, who founded Dublin's first cinema, keeps more than one projector running.

"Katey and Boody Dedalus shoved in the door of the close steaming kitchen." They are the sisters of Stephen, and the daughters of feckless Simon. They live at Number Seven, St. Peter's Terrace, Cabra, where they boil shirts and lament their lack of money, even though they have just pawned Stephen's books. Another sister, Dilly, has gone to meet their "father who are not in heaven" to get money. The artist on home ground – in June 1904 the Joyce family lived in tumult and penury at Number Seven, St. Peter's Terrace, Cabra.

Blazes Boylan, Bloom's cuckoldiser has gone into Thornton's the fruit shop at Sixty-Three, Grafton Street, to order some fruit to be sent ahead – to "somebody". While he ogles the "young pullet" bosom of a blond girl, "H.E.L.Y.'S. filed before him, tallwhitehatted". He asks to use the telephone.

Stephen has walked from the library down Kildare Street, turned left into Nassau Street and then to College Green and the statues in front of Trinity. Carrying his ashplant walking stick, he meets Almidano Artifoni, his singing-master, under "Goldsmith's knobby poll". Another pun? "Here lies Oliver Goldsmith More often called Noll Who wrote like an angel But talked like poor Poll", was the poet's own epitaph. Poll? Parrot? Head? In name, Almidano Artifoni was the principal at the Trieste Berlitz Institute, who gave Joyce a teaching job. In character, he was the Jesuit Father, Charles Ghezzi, who taught Joyce Dante.

The phone rings in Boylan's house of business at Number Fifteen, D'Olier Street, just around the corner from where Stephen is. The message passes on the wires somewhere in the air above and near Stephen; he is between Boylan in Grafton Street and Boylan's secretary in D'Olier Street. Miss Dunne's conversation with Mr. Boylan closes with the words that he is to meet Mr. Lenehan at the Ormond Hotel at four. The citizens of *Ulysses* are on the move.

J. J. O'Molloy is a Dublin gurrier – in low common parlance he only leaves his street corner or bar stool to cadge. Now he comes to Ned Lambert in the chapterhouse of Mary's Abbey, finds Ned at work showing a clergyman, the Reverend Hugh C. Love, the vaulted arches of the old chapterhouse: "We are standing in the historic council chamber of

Saint Mary's Abbey where silken Thomas proclaimed himself a rebel in 1534."

Had you been standing on O'Connell Bridge between the hours of three and four o'clock on that faraway Thursday afternoon nothing would have appeared different. But nothing was different: all these citizens were only doing what they did every day. They came, stayed, went, and the commonest acts of man became the brush-strokes on Joyce's canvas, the detail in his portrait of everyman.

Tom Rochford is displaying a machine he has invented to tell theatre latecomers which variety act is on. Richie Goulding, Stephen's cousin, is on his professional way to the courts across the river. Lenehan and M'Coy walk out of Crampton Court and into the labyrinth between Dame Street and the river, on their way to the Ormond Hotel to meet Boylan at four o'clock. A stop at the bookmakers, praise for Tom Rochford who saved a man from a sewer, what about the Gold Cup?

> They went up the steps and under Merchants' Arch. A darkbacked figure scanned books on the hawker's cart.
> There he is, Lenehan said.
> Wonder what he is buying. M'Coy said, glancing behind.
> Leopoldo or the Bloom is on the Rye, Lenehan said.

The wandering Jew – whom they discuss. Bloom's hobby is astronomy: "he's a cultured allroundman Bloom is". The two worthies walk from Crampton Court to Dame Street, Sycamore Street, Essex Street and Temple Bar.

At breakfast Molly asked Mr. Bloom to get her a book. "Get another of Paul de Kock's. Nice name he has." There is still a book barrow at Merchants' Arch. "*Sweets of Sin*, he said, tapping on it. That's a good one." And on O'Connell Bridge "many persons observed the grave deportment and gay apparel of Mr. Denis J. Maginni, professor of dancing".

On Bachelor's Walk, directly across the river, Dilly Dedalus stands in wait for her father Simon. Deflecting, Mr. Dedalus urges her not to slouch and abusively tries to straighten her shoulders. After his wife died and was buried in Glasnevin, John Joyce treated his family appallingly, too. "I'll break your bloody heart," he used to yell, "I'll break your stomach first, ye buggers." Now, Dilly insists that Simon Dedalus has more money than the shilling he hands over. Eventually, because she grins at his joke, he surrenders two pennies more. And at this moment "the viceregal cavalcade passed, greeted by obsequious policemen, out of Parkgate".

The St. James's Gate brewery of Arthur Guinness and Company was, in Joyce's time, the biggest in the world. Mr. Kernan walks towards it: on the way he preens himself in the sloping mirror of Peter Kennedy, hairdresser, at Forty-Eight, James's Street. He thinks he sees Ned Lambert's brother Sam "over the way". But the sun flashes in the windscreen of a motor-car and he is not sure. Who is Mr. Kernan? You may as well ask who is Ned Lambert? And his brother Sam? Who is J. J. O'Molloy, Tom Rochford, Mrs. Breen, M'Coy, Lenehan, the one-legged sailor? People, citizens of Dublin, Joycean corpuscles. And as Mr. Kernan turned down Watling Street "by the corner of Guinness' visitors' waitingroom", Mrs. Breen, who lately had a conversation with Mr. Bloom, goes over O'Connell Bridge, half a mile away, with her husband who is not the full shilling. "A cavalcade in easy trot along Pembroke quay passed, outriders leaping, leaping in their, in their saddles. Frockcoats. Cream sunshades."

In Bedford Row "Stephen Dedalus watched through the webbed window the lapidary's fingers prove a timedulled chain". In Clohissey's window "a faded 1860 print of Heenan boxing Sayers held his eye". Mr. Bloom is a few minutes away, in Merchants' Arch, book-buying.

Stephen, too – in Bedford Row, still – "turned and halted by the slanted bookcart". Perhaps he will see and re-purchase some of the "schoolprizes" his hungry sisters pawned. Could they still be there, on today's bookcarts? Oh – the temptation to look for a flyleaved "S. Dedalus, 1904". Dilly comes forward to Stephen bearing shyly a coverless *Chardeual's French Primer*. She blushes when he wrings from her that she spent one of her pennies on it to learn French.

The picture hangs. Stephen – at a book-barrow in one of the little streets, his scrawny sister standing before him: Bloom – bent "darkbacked" over another barrow around the corner: Lenehan and M'Coy walking past, clouds scudding slow across the sky, the viceregal cavalcade clip-clopping along the quays.

Simon Dedalus meets "Father" Cowley outside the premises of Reddy and Daughters on Ormond Quay where they "clasped hands loudly". Cowley complains that Reuben J. Dodd, the moneylender, has two bailiffs pursuing him. But who can approach the subsheriff and have the bailiffs hauled off? Aha! "Ben Dollard's loose blue cutaway and square hat above large slops crossed the quay in full gait from the metal bridge."

"The youngster will be all right, Martin Cunningham said, as they passed out of the Castleyard Gate", the youngster being poor Dignam's son. The mourners have convened to care for the bereaved. "Yes, Martin Cunningham said, fingering his beard. I wrote to Father Conmee and laid the whole case before him." From the gate of Dublin Castle to Kavanagh's winerooms at Twenty-Seven, Parliament Street is but a short journey, around the corner and down the hill. Martin Cunningham is making the trip – to see the subsheriff, Long John Fanning, about the case of the Dignams. "Horses pass Parliament Street, harness and glossy posterns in sunlight glimmering."

"As they trod across the thick carpet Buck Mulligan whispered behind his panama to Haines. 'Parnell's brother. There in the corner'." The Buck has parted company with Stephen and is about to take tea at the Dublin Bakery Company's tearooms, Thirty-Five, Dame Street. Haines and Mulligan order *mélanges* and scones and butter and cakes. The Buck chuckles: "We call it D.B.C. because they have damn bad cakes." Cashel Boyle O'Connor Fitzmaurice Tisdall Farrell is outside the lampposts of Merrion Square a mile away, behind him the blind stripling whom Bloom guided earlier, before him, Almidano Artifoni, homegoing. The characters walk in each other's footsteps, in a long-stretched straight line, by the walls of College Park, along Nassau Street, South Leinster Street and Clare Street into Merrion Square and ahead as far as Mount Street.

"Opposite Ruggy O'Donohoe's Master Patrick Aloysius Dignam, pawing the pound and half of Mangan's, late Fehrenbach's, porksteaks he had been sent for, went along warm Wicklow Street dawdling."

Bored with the mourners sitting in the parlour, he

goes to get the bidden meat. Master Dignam sees a poster in a window advertising a boxing match. "Myler Keogh, Dublin's pet lamb, will meet sergeantmajor Bennett, the Portobello bruiser, for a purse of fifty sovereigns" and Master Dignam contemplates on how much he would like to see that match. But he notices with chagrin that the date on the poster is May the twentysecond. "Sure, the blooming thing is all over." "In Grafton Street Master Dignam saw a red flower in a toff's mouth and a swell pair of kicks on him." Blazes Boylan, none other. Master Dignam continues his slow schoolboy's journey into Nassau Street.

Four o'clock approaches and there is sunlight and warm air and soft clouds. Pause. Let us not be boggled by this dazzling chess-player, Joyce, let us survey the board.

An hour ago play commenced when Father John Conmee set off on a journey to get a boy into a school, a mercy inspired by Martin Cunningham who shared a funeral carriage with Mr. Bloom and Mr. Dedalus and Mr. Power.

Professor Maginni is dancing, the five whitehatted H.E.L.Y.'S. sandwichmen are eeling, through the city. Corny Kelleher, the undertaker, spits. A one-legged sailor, blessed by Father Conmee, fetches the coin thrown by Molly Bloom. The Dedalus sisters are burning books to boil shirts. Blazes Boylan buys fruit for "someone", telephones his secretary. Stephen Dedalus meets his kind singing teacher, Almidano Artifoni. Lenehan tells M'Coy stories about Molly Bloom. J. J. O'Molloy tries to borrow money from Ned Lambert who is showing a historic building to the Reverend Hugh C. Love. Bob Cowley is off fending the Reverend Hugh C. Love's bailiffs, Simon Dedalus is fending off his equally distraining daughter. Under Merchants' Arch, near Lenehan and M'Coy, Mr. Bloom obtains *Sweets of Sin*, a book for his

wife. Mr. Kernan gleams at his reflection in a barber's looking-glass. Father Conmee blesses gravely a young couple who come flushed through the hedge. Martin Cunningham talks to the sub-sheriff, Long John Fanning, about the relatives of the late poor Dignam. Buck Mulligan and Haines see Parnell's brother in a teashop. Cashel Boyle what's-his-name bumps into a blind youth. Master Dignam, unknowing of Jews and Blooms, buys porksteaks.

Through the glittering green valleys of the Phoenix Park "William Humble, Earl of Dudley, and Lady Dudley, accompanied by lieutenantcolonel Hesseltine, drove out after luncheon from the viceregal lodge. In the following carriage were the honourable Mrs. Paget, Miss de Courcy and the honourable Gerald Ward, A.D.C., in attendance", along the long Liffey quays, by bridges to Parliament Street, Dame Street, College Green and Nassau Street – to Sandymount, to open the Mirus Bazaar in aid of funds for Mercer's Hospital. Dublin salutes the Viceroy – one way and another. On Ormond Quay Simon Dedalus gestures rudely. The Reverend Hugh C. Love's greeting goes unperceived, because he is out of sight. Lenehan and M'Coy look from Grattan/Essex Bridge.

Tom Rochford doffs his cap. Buck Mulligan and Haines, eating Damn Bad Cakes in Dame Street, look gaily and gravely down. Dilly Dedalus sees "sunshades spanned and wheelspokes spinning in the glare" of Fownes's Street. In Dame Street poor Mr. Breen is hauled from under the cavalcade wheels by his wife. The H.E.L.Y.'S., tallwhitehatted, come to a halt in Grafton Street. Mr. Denis J. Maginni pays absolutely no attention in Westmoreland Street. Blazes Boylan acknowledges, at the wall of the Provost's house, in "a skyblue tie, a widebrimmed straw hat at a rakish angle and a suit of indigo serge". Cashel Boyle and-so-forth turns back along Clare Street defiant in the opposite direction. Master Dignam "raised his new black cap". The blind stripling listens to the cavalcade on Mount Street. And Signor Artifoni goes through the door of his home, Number Fourteen Lansdowne Road.

SIRENS

Jingling, cleartinkling music and strong song rises on the sighing afternoon. Over the bridges and down the cobbled quays you may meet singers and golden liquids in a sunbeamed, dim, woodgrained bar.

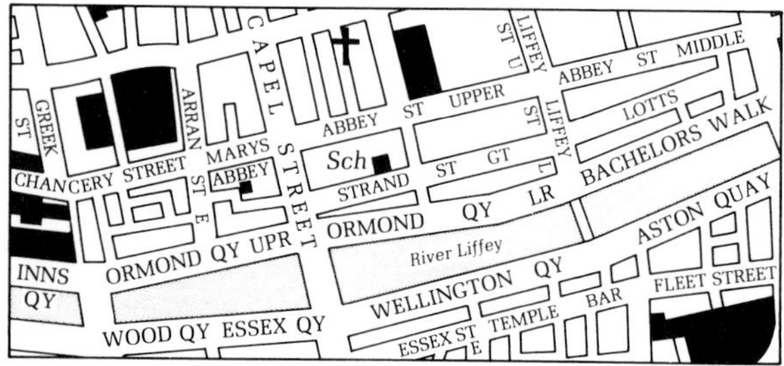

"Bronze by gold, Miss Douce's head by Miss Kennedy's head, over the crossblind of the Ormond Bar heard the viceregal hoofs go by." The two barmaids in the Ormond Hotel had been watching the progress of the viceregal cavalcade as it sped by the Liffey. Miss Douce's head was the colour of bronze, Miss Kennedy's head was the colour of gold and they were lively, vulgar young things. They were excited by the passing silk and grey of the cavalcade and when they left the window to resume duty on their island behind the bar the insolent Boots served them tea. "They cowered under their reef of counter, waiting on footstools, crates upturned, waiting for their teas to draw. They pawed their blouses, both of black satin, two and nine a yard, waiting for their teas to draw, and two and seven."

The barmaids lured the men of the city to their reefs at the bar of the Ormond Hotel. The Sirens were beautiful to the waist but in the lower regions had the bodies of birds, from the neck down, or the tails of fish from the waist down. Miss Kennedy and Miss Douce looked pristine and angelic when seen at the height of a bar counter, but their skirts and footwear were much shabbier than their black satin blouses and bronzegold features.

The Ormond Hotel still stands on a Liffey Quay. It has undergone considerable renovations since 1904 but parts of the old hotel are still to be seen. The panelling in the dining-room is of the colour and fabric which Joyce knew; at the back, some as yet unrenovated, used for meetings now, are the very rooms in which the singing of the Sirens took place. Outside, the river view has not changed. Downstream, stared at by the half-lidded eyes of many bridges, the considered skyline is gently jagged, scalloped, by the domes of churches, the squares of warehouses, the minaret of a malting tower and the narrowing tallness of an occasional residence. Lowering windows, warping sashes, upstairs musty apartments, old offices: below, the old shops still serve country customers. The Liffey is untroubled here, the line of its containing rampart is even, unbroken – save for the arched bridges and hanging tongues of piped water. Churches face each

other: and in a final agreement between Church and State the Franciscans and the Four Courts, green-domed and austere, sentry the stream.

The parallel quays palpitate the city. Inwards, with the river's tide, the veins: from Kingsbridge, past Usher's Island and Merchants' Arch come the new citizens, to O'Connell Bridge. On the opposite side, against the tide, the artery of Bachelor's Walk, the Four Courts, the Ormond Hotel, the way home to the west, past Kingsbridge, past Islandbridge, Phoenix Park, Chapelizod, the road for drovers, dealers and their goods and cattle, the way to *Finnegans Wake*.

When Joyce had finished writing the "Sirens" he lost all interest in music for a time. He had put so much into the chapter, in the notes, chords and contrapuntals of the prose, that he felt had it all been drained out of his system. As a boy he sang sweetly, as a man, publicly. He appeared on the same concert platform as the celebrated tenor John McCormack, he came second in Dublin's premier singing competition – and threw the medal away, disgusted both at losing, and at not being able to pawn it. But his singing performances were reviewed by the newspapers. After he appeared on the 27th of August, 1904 in a Grand Irish Concert at the Antient (sic) Concert Rooms, now the Academy Cinema on Pearse Street, the *Freeman's Journal* wrote:

"Mr. James A. Joyce, the possessor of a sweet tenor voice, sang charmingly 'The Sally Gardens' and gave a pathetic rendering of 'The Croppy Boy'." Another critic wrote: "Mr. Joyce possesses a light tenor voice, which he is inclined to force on the high notes but he sings with artistic emotionalism." Nora often said he should have stuck to the singing.

Ulysses had been warned that the sweet song of the Sirens would lure, had lured, all mortal men to

their deaths on the ferocious island of the Sirens. He sealed the ears of his companions with wax and lashed himself to the mast in order to resist the temptation. Behind the counter of the Ormond Hotel Miss Douce and Miss Kennedy greet a variety of men who wander in. As the afternoon shines on, one man departs, lured by another Siren, others stay: soon, sweet sounds, lóng notes, come from the concert-room.

The first strolling player is Simon Dedalus, father of the bard. He hoped Miss Douce had nice holiday weather in Rostrevor.

> Gorgeous, she said. Look at the holy show I am. Lying out on the strand all day.
>
> Bronze whiteness.
>
> That was exceedingly naughty of you, Mr. Dedalus told her and pressed her hand indulgently. Tempting poor simple males.
>
> Miss Douce of satin douced her arm away.
>
> O go away, she said. You're very simple, I don't think.

The next arrival is Lenehan, looking for Blazes Boylan. He informs Mr. Dedalus that Stephen has earlier had the elite of Erin hanging on his lips while he drank with the newspapermen in Mooneys.

And Mr. Bloom is still wandering. He has crossed the river at Essex Bridge, bought "two sheets cream vellum paper one reserve two envelopes" to reply to Martha's letter. As he emerges from the shop, eye falling on a poster with a mermaid advertising cigarettes, Mr. Bloom's heart stops again. "He eyed and saw afar on Essex Bridge a gay hat riding on a jauntingcar. It is. Third time. Coincidence." Blazes Boylan is on his way to the Ormond Hotel to meet Lenehan. Then he has an appointment at Number Seven, Eccles Street, with

Mrs. Marion Bloom, as per the letter she received from him that morning.

Dublin in 1904 heard many songs. The music-hall soldiery loved Victorian drawing-room ballads. All classes and creeds – who could afford it – went to the opera. The ceaseless flow of international operatic stars through Dublin was always assured of an attentive audience. Once, a visiting tenor in *La Traviata* was unable to resume, by dint of beverage, in the second act. "Ladies and gentlemen," apologised the manager, "I regret to announce that our tenor will not be appearing in Act Two. He is, I'm afraid, suffering an attack of malaria." A raucous voice from the pit yelled: "Malaria! Jaysus! I'd love a bottle of that meself."

In the Ormond Hotel, "from the saloon a call came, long in dying. That was a tuning-fork the tuner had that he forgot that he now struck. A call again. That he now poised that it throbbed. You hear? It throbbed, pure, purer, softly and softlier, its buzzing prongs. Longer in dying call." Lured to the Ormond Hotel, "Blazes Boylan's smart tan shoes creaked on the barfloor where he strode", greeted by barmaids and Lenehan. The poor nervous Mr. Bloom, aware that Boylan is about to visit Molly, slips unseen into the dining-room while in the concert-room "a voiceless song sang from within".

Three levels of awareness – Mr. Bloom on the outside, not wanting to see Boylan, able to hear the unseen song. At the bar "Boylan bespoke potions"; Mr. Bloom ordered liver and bacon; deep inside the inner ear the Ormond rang with song.

Richard Ellman quotes James Joyce's conversation with a friend on the 18th of June, 1919.

> I finished the "Sirens" chapter during the last few days. A big job. I wrote this chapter with the technical resources of music. It is a fugue with all

musical notations: piano, forte, rallentando, and so on. A quintet occurs in it too, as in *Die Meistersinger*, my favourite Wagnerian opera . . . Since exploring the resources and artifices of music and employing them in this chapter, I haven't cared for music any more. I, the great friend of music, can no longer listen to it. I see through all the tricks and can't enjoy it any more.

Ellmann tells too, the story of Joyce reading "Sirens" to a friend just before they left for *Die Walküre*. At the interval Joyce asked the friend, an enthusiastic Wagnerian, whether he didn't think that the musical efforts of "Sirens" were better than Wagner's? When the friend disagreed Joyce departed in a huff.

A different kind of music is organised from Miss Douce. "Smack. She let free sudden in rebound her nipped elastic garter smackwarm against her smackable woman's warmhosed thigh" to the vast amusement of Blazes and acolyte Lenehan. "Boylan eyed, eyed. Tossed to fat lips his chalice, drankoff his tiny chalice, sucking the last fat violet syrupy drops." Blazes Boylan departed for his appointment. Poor Mr. Bloom. "Bloom heard a jing, a little sound. He's off. Light sob of breath." The tension, the lust rises. "By Bachelor's Walk jogjaunty jingled Blazes Boylan, bachelor, in sun, in heat, mare's glossy rump atrot, with a flick of whip, on bounding tyres: sprawled, warmseated, Boylan impatience, ardentbold." And back at the Ormond Hotel, like a sound-track, barreltoned Ben Dollard's voice booms: "When love absorbs my ardent soul . . ." Blazes Boylan the impressario, and Mrs. Marion Bloom are about to rehearse "Love's Old Sweet Song". Joyce was attracted/repelled by the notion that Nora was attractive to other men – despite her fidelity to him. But when a journalist in Trieste called Prezioso, whose friendship Joyce encouraged, wanted Nora to become his mistress, Joyce tonguelashed him to tears.

"In liver gravy Bloom mashed mashed potatoes." It is just past four o'clock. Mr. Bloom sits at the table "married in silence" to Richie Goulding who has ordered steak and kidney pie, all brought by Pat the bald, deaf waiter. Within, watched by Miss Douce and Miss Kennedy, there is to be a splendid singing. The piano is now in tune, thanks to a certain blind stripling who came this morning but left his tuning fork behind him. Came Simon Dedalus' voice:

> It soared like a bird, it held its flight, a swift pure cry, soar silver orb it leaped serene, speeding, sustained, to come, don't spin it out too long long breath he breath long life, soaring high, high resplendent, aflame, crowned, high in the effulgence symbolistic, high, of the ethereal bosom, high of the vast irradiation everywhere all soaring all around about the all, the endlessnessnessness . . .

"Sirens" has often been described as the most beautiful episode in *Ulysses*. It represents the ear, and all through the chapter, songs and sounds resound like various sections of an orchestra. Even the opening passages are shaped like an overture, tiny quotes and phrases dotted and pitched across the page, notes for the fuller chords to come. Then the sounds of the afternoon – the recurring jingle of Boylan's jauntingcar matching the jingling brass quoits on Molly's bed of brass, the tap-tap-tapping of the blind stripling coming back for his tuning-fork, the clap-clap-clapping which greeted each song sung, the "cockcarracarra" rat-tat-tat-tat of Boylan with the doorknocker of Number Seven, Eccles Street.

Ben Dollard stands up to sing "The Croppy Boy", a song of betrayal. Mr. Bloom writes to

"Martha Clifford c/o P.O. Dolphin's Barn Lane Dublin". Miss Lydia Douce displays the shell she brought back from holiday. Bob Cowley plays the piano in F sharp major. Blazes Boylan knocks on Molly's door and she titivates lingeringly in the hall mirror before opening up. The blind stripling piano-tuner tap-taps his way down the quays. Lonely, Mr. Bloom leaves the music of the Ormond Hotel.

While Joyce was writing the *Sirens* he went with a friend to Locarno. He had heard of an old baroness who made dolls on an island in Lake Maggiore. She was known locally as the Siren because she lived a curious life on her little isle and was reputed to have buried seven husbands. Clearly she embraced her nickname; she had the walls of her rooms decorated with Homeric themes. Joyce wrote to her à propos his own *Ulysses*, requesting a viewing of her pictures. She invited him to the island where she gave him access to a chest full of obscene letters and erotic books.

"A frowsy whore with a black sailor hat askew came glazily in the day along the quay towards Mr. Bloom." He is so lonely, so lonely, trying to keep the pictures of Blazes and Molly out of his mind, but on a previous assignation the whore mentioned Molly," stout lady does be with you in the brown costume". So lonely Mr. Bloom turns instead to a shop window, and introverts himself into the lanes, burrows and furrows behind the Ormond Hotel.

CYCLOPS

Surrounded by echoes of previous patriots, the policemen at Green Street Court protect the city and the world from rebellious sentiment. The ruined corner by Barney Kiernan's pub is cordoned by slogans taken down and used in evidence.

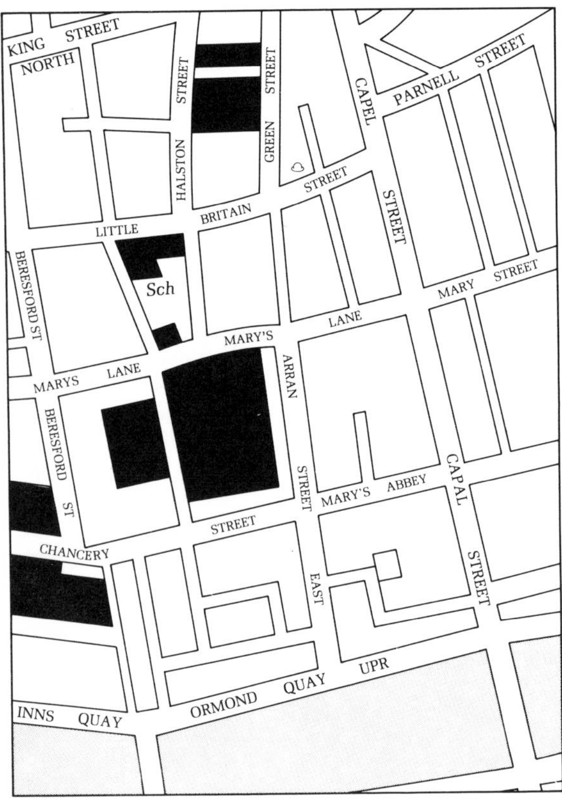

A nameless narrator, after a brief conversation with Constable Troy of the Dublin Metropolitan Police, an altercation with the bristles of a chimneysweep, an encounter with a friend, is on his way to Barney Kiernan's pub in Little Britain Street for the most savagely satirical chapter in *Ulysses*. The time is five o'clock in the afternoon: Barney Kiernan's pub is now vanished, a dying parish by Green Street Courthouse, in the heart of the markets.

I was just passing the time of day with old Troy of the D.M.P. at the corner of Arbour Hill there and be damned but a boody old sweep came along and he near drove his gear into my eye. I turned around to let him have the weight of my tongue when who should I see dodging along Stony Batter only Joe Hynes.

Lo, Joe, says I. How are you blowing? Did you see that bloody chimneysweep near shove my eye out with his brush?

Mr. Bloom is wandering somewhere in the dingy labyrinth between Ormond Quay and Little Britain Street. He has agreed to meet Martin Cunningham at the Courthouse in order to establish a charitable fund for the relatives of poor Dignam. He has purchased a postal order gift for Martha, and a stamp: needing solitude he walks sadly into the warren of streets on his way to five o'clock. In these streets the pubs have always had special licensing laws to open in the early morning hours of the markets, a special tipple is poured. Old Dublin still clings, small houses, broken terraces, sparse now. Citizens here are unto the second and third generation, do not want to leave. But an old person living alone falls ill, is moved to hospital, never returns and the dead house is boarded up. Eventually it is incorporated into town planning.

The style of "Cyclops" is garrulous and malicious: the narrator adopts a pretence of friendship and familiarity sufficiently ingratiating to encourage free drink. An old Irish pastime: at funerals unfamiliar wellwishers were a familiar sight, offering condolence in exchange for drink at

the wake. Sometimes they were disappointed. Once, near my home, a regular was chagrined at the dryness of the house. Days later when queried as to "What did poor Mr. Hogan die of?" this "mourner" snorted: "Drought." In the bar of Barney Kiernan's sits "the citizen up in the corner having a great confab with himself and that bloody mangy mongrel, Garryowen, and he waiting for what the sky would drop in the way of drink". Enter the citizen, the central character in "Cyclops".

By the time Joyce left Dublin in 1904 he was convinced that his fellow citizens were the most malicious, priest-ridden, treacherous, calumnious, politically dubious, devious breed. He was the deer, the antlered intellect, the nervous, elegant animal – his countrymen were the hounds, ready, anxious to tear him down. It was his favourite image of his young self – but was he aware of his own emotional and social malice, his multifarious, unrestituted borrowings, his tidal contempt for every living Irish writer?

"So begob the citizen claps his paw on his knee and he says: Foreign wars is the cause of it." Ulysses fought the one-eyed giant, Cyclops. The citizen can only see the Irish Question from one nationalistic point of view. He is entirely blind to the view of somebody who doesn't believe that "The Cause" is all, he is blind to all other points of view, to reason, to logic. It is a literary irony that Barney Kiernan's pub stood on a corner across from Green Street Courthouse, which for a decade and more has been the venue for those on trial for politically-claimed crimes. And Joyce calls up the old, old images, the legends, the stuff of slogans: ". . . Cuchulin, Conn of hundred battles, Niall of nine hostages, Brian of Kincora, the Ardri Malachi. Art MacMurragh, Shane O'Neill, Father John Murphy, Owen Roe, Patrick Sarsfield, Red Hugh O'Donnell. Red Jim McDermott . . ." and on, and on, and on until the ludicrous emerges . . . ". . . the Mother of the Maccabees, the Last of the Mohicans, the Rose of Castille, the Man for Galway, the Man that Broke the Bank at Monte Carlo, the Man in the Gap, the Woman who Didn't . . ."

It is only five o'clock but this is Dublin and there are plenty of conversationalists in the pub. "What's that bloody freemason doing, says the citizen, prawling up and down outside?" Mr. Bloom is waiting for his appointment. A minor civil servant produces a batch of letters, applications for the post of hangman. One is signed "H. Rumbold". In Zurich in 1918 Joyce had a violent disagreement with the British diplomatic authorities whose Minister to Switzerland was Sir Horace Rumbold. Joyce later referred to him as "Sir Whorearse Rumhole"; two of his staff, Gann and Smith, appear as hanged murderers in the hangman's application.

> There he is again, says the citizen, staring out.
> Who? says I.
> Bloom, says he. He's on point duty up and down there for the last ten minutes.
> And, begob, I saw his physog do a peep in and then slidder off again.

There was endless conversation in the Joyce household, as often as not politics, Parnell's fall from grace – and because of a woman! – was a sore point with Joyce's father whose every drink mourned the ivy leaf, Parnell's symbol. At University, books, literature, theology and the destiny of man prevailed. In Trieste and Zurich and Paris there were long, long hours of café conversation: the slim figure with the thick, disconcerting spectacles drank coffee when his wife was there, absinthe and anything when she was not. Since alcohol affected, aggravated, his appalling eye

JAMESON

AN CHUIRT

troubles – over a dozen operations – she looked unkindly on any visitor who might tempt him. And testimony exists to the rowdiness of her welcome if he came home intoxicated. Mr. Bloom is offered a drink: "he wouldn't and couldn't and excuse him no offence and all to that and then he said well he'd just take a cigar. Gob, he's a prudent member and no mistake."

Arthur Griffith, founder of Sinn Fein, editor of the *United Irishman,* signatory of the 1921 Anglo-Irish Treaty was born on Little Britain Street.

In Green Street Courthouse they tried Young Irelanders, Fenians, I.R.A., Invincibles, Robert Emmet, "the darling of Erin", the Sheares Brothers; patriotism in the dock. Joyce modelled the Citizen on Michael Cusack, the patriot who founded the Gaelic Athletic Association, Ireland's largest sporting body; Joyce had met the ineluctably patriotic Cusack, found him narrow-minded, was delighted to dislike him intensely.

> And the citizen and Bloom having an argument about the point, the brothers Sheares and Wolfe Tone beyond on Arbour Hill and Robert Emmet and die for your country, the Tommy Moore touch about Sara Curran and she's far from the land. And Bloom, of course, with his knockmedown cigar putting on swank with his lardy face.

The Cyclops was blinded when a stake was stabbed in his one eye.

"So anyhow in came John Wyse Nolan and Lenehan with him with a face on him as long as a late breakfast. Well, says the citizen, what's the latest from the scene of the action?" "Throwaway", twenty to one, won the Gold Cup, much recrimination, regret.

Mr. Bloom's friends still haven't arrived, he goes in search.

A Dublin saying: if you value your repute, never leave a group of three or more. And sure enough:

> Isn't that a fact, says John Wyse, what I was telling the citizen about Bloom and the Sinn Fein?
> That's so, says Martin. Or so they allege.
> Who made those allegations? says Alf.
> I, says Joe. I'm the alligator.
> And after all, says John Wyse, why can't a jew love his country like the next fellow?

Mr. Bloom has offered Arthur Griffith some neutral political advice – but much more serious is the idea that he may have made money on "Throwaway" and gone to collect it. They believe it may even be five pounds, that Bloom won't tell them lest he has to buy a drink. "Do you know what I'm telling you? It'd be an act of God to take hold of a fellow the like of that and throw him in the bloody sea. Justifiable homicide, so it would. Then sloping off with his five quid without putting up a pint of stuff like a man."

The citizen represents all that Joyce hated about his fellow man. He is a characterless scrounger, good for nothing except drink and calumny, without a good word to say for anybody alive, capable only of looking for and seeing the worst in everybody, suspicious, narrow-minded and dogmatic,

thriving on the mishaps of others and all too willing to recount them – a loud-mouthed, opinionated, unfair, unsporting, bigoted, cant-carrying, know-all. When Joyce's own enemies drew their own portrait of the artist, he seemed not unlike the citizen.

Martin Cunningham smells trouble. The citizen has the courage of drink and rage on him. Mr. Bloom is eased out to the jauntingcar that will take them to Dignam's widow in Sandymount. The citizen rushes out. There is a ferocious verbal altercation, with the citizen hurling abuse at Mr. Bloom, mainly aimed at his Jewishness. Mr. Bloom as usual tries to reason the point: "Your God was a jew. Christ was a jew like me. Gob, the citizen

made a plunge back into the shop. By Jesus, says he, I'll brain that bloody jewman for using the holy name. By Jesus, I'll crucify him, so I will", and he hurls a biscuit tin after the departing jauntingcar, while the citizen's dog, Garryowen, pursues ineffectually.

> The catastrophe was terrific and instantaneous in its effect. The observatory of Dunsink registered in all eleven shocks, all of the fifth grade of Mercalli's scale, and there is no record extant of a similar seismic disturbance in our island since the earthquake of 1534, the year of the rebellion of Silken Thomas.

In "Cyclops", Ireland is a land where shining palaces rise with crystal glittering roofs: "The figure seated on a large boulder at the foot of a round tower was that of a broadshouldered deepchested stronglimbed frankeyed redhaired freely freckled shaggybearded widemouthed largenosed longheaded deepvoiced barekneed brawnyhanded hairylegged ruddyfaced sinewyarmed hero." At a mythical hanging, to lampoon friend Rumbold further, "a word of praise is due to the Little Sisters of the Poor for their excellent idea of affording the good fatherless and motherless children a genuinely instructive treat". The Catholic Church – against whom Joyce railed for ever – doesn't escape: ". . . S. Denis and S. Cornelius and S. Leopold and S. Bernard and S. Terence and S. Edward and S. Owen Caniculus and S. Anonymous and S. Eponymous and S. Pseudonymous and S. Homonymous and S. Paronymous and S. Synonymous . . ."

Joyce said once, not without sadness, to Nora: "The pity is the public will demand and find a moral in my book, or worse, they may take it in some serious way, and on the honour of a gentleman, there is not one serious single line in it."

NAUSICAA

*The sun set on Bloomsday at twenty-
seven minutes past eight
and its undertaking shadows wrapped
the rocks of Sandymount Strand in
deep purple thought.*

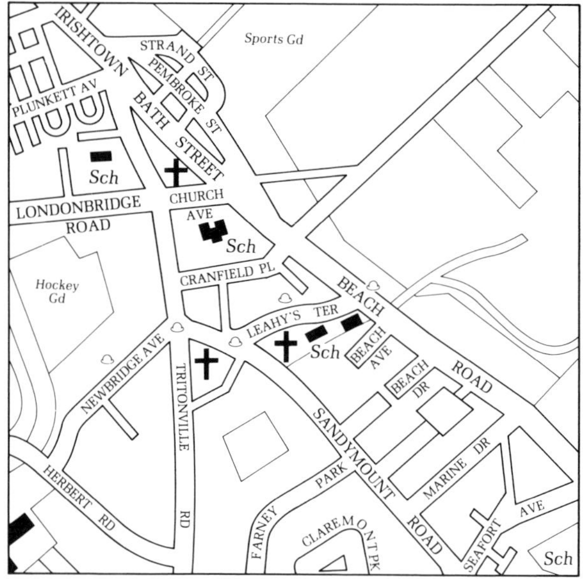

Sandymount was a resort then, where men bathed naked and old women sold crabs and cockles from hand-held, homeweave baskets to the strollers. It was broad and bright and within sufficiently easy reach of Dublin for the men of heart and quality to maintain mistresses there. In the distance Howth Head lay, snout to the waves like a farrowing sow. Carriages and horsemen clopped by; at that hour of the evening the last businessmen were coming home to Blackrock and Kingstown. Nearby the noise of a train perhaps, sparks lighting the fireman's face?

Mr. Bloom saw, at that gathering hour, three girls sitting on the rocks, caring the while for curlyheaded four-year-old twin boys and a baby in a pushchair. Mr. Bloom has just completed his errand of mercy to Mrs. Dignam at Newbridge Avenue nearby; poor Dignam's policy is to be straightened out and paid over. Then, as Stephen did at noon, he walked on to Sandymount Strand via Leahy's Terrace.

On Sandymount Strand now, the twin red-and-white towers of the Pigeon House are studded with red flashing lights to warn aircraft. Cars bound by, both ways; the lights of the bay form a horseshoe to Howth. The summer evening is calm upon the lovers walking the sands, the last sunlight shafts the terraces and churches along the shore to Seapoint, to the smoke-plumed mailboat at Dun Laoire and inevitably to the round shadow of the Martello Tower in Sandycove.

Leopold Bloom comes to Sandymount to gather himself, to take away the pain of the day. His watch, he finds, stopped at half past four – the moment of conjunction between Molly and Boylan? "Was that just when he, she?"

In the holy time breathless with adoration litanies are said in a nearby church. Cissy Caffrey and Edy Boardman are looking after Tommy and Jacky Caffrey and Baby Boardman and Gerty MacDowell is looking on, gently aloof.

Her figure was slight and graceful, inclining even to fragility but those iron jelloids she had been taking of

late had done her a world of good much better than the Widow Welch's female pills and she was much better of those discharges she used to get and that tired feeling. The waxen pallor of her face was almost spiritual in its ivorylike purity though her rosebud mouth was a genuine Cupid's bow, Greekly perfect. Her hands were of finely veined alabaster with tapering fingers and as white as lemon juice and queen of ointments could make them thought it was not true that she used to wear kid gloves in bed or take a milk footbath either. Bertha Supple told that once to Edy Boardman, a deliberate lie, when she was black out at daggers drawn with Gerty . . .

The slight action of "Nausicaa" is overwhelming on several levels. In the nearby church, the organ pealed during the men's temperance retreat while "still the voices rang in supplication to the Virgin most powerful, Virgin most merciful". Gerty MacDowell dreams of love and a boy she knows. Leaning back upon the rocks, half-consciously she allows Mr. Bloom see her underwear:

> four dinky sets, with awfully pretty stitchery, three garments and nighties extra, and each set slotted with different coloured ribbons, rosepink, pale blue, mauve and peagreen and she aired them herself and blued them when they came home from the wash and ironed them and she had a brickbat to keep the iron on because she wouldn't trust those washerwomen as far as she'd see them scorching the things.

As Mr. Bloom sees her thighs, the fireworks display at the bazaar, opened earlier by the viceroy, burst a Roman candle in the sky "and it was like a sigh of O! and everyone cried O! O! in raptures and it gushed out of it a stream of rain gold hair threads and they shed and ah!" Mr. Bloom, excited, has become his own Roman candle; and now he "stands silent, with bowed head before those young guileless eyes. What a brute he had been! At it again?" Gerty MacDowell, by some sweet telepathy, suspects what it is Mr. Bloom has been at and never having spoken, or moved closer than some yards, she walks sadly away giving him "a sweet forgiving smile, a smile that verged on tears, and then they parted". Mr. Bloom notices that she is lame, thinks she is pre-menstrual and wonders about women in general and, it has to be said, in particular too. In the church the devotions have ended.

One day, late in 1918 – he lived in Zurich then and was almost thirty-seven-years-old – James Joyce walked home to his flat behind a dark-haired, dark-eyed young woman who had a slight limp. He was electrified. He watched her go into her house and discovered she lived around the corner from him. Her name was Martha Fleischmann, she was Swiss, conceited, and kept by an engineer. Joyce prevailed upon her, wrote to her, watched her from his own windows, was moved passionately by her and in his mind at least – for she was not so forthcoming – had a sizzling affair with her.

On his thirty-seventh birthday, the 2nd of February, 1919, she agreed to allow him call on her, which he did bearing a borrowed ceremonial candlestick, for it was Candlemas Day. What transpired in the glow? Neither said – but they did not meet again for some time. Their correspondence ended, too; Martha's jealous lover (who was, after all, paying the bills) found out.

Gerty MacDowell must have been based on Martha Fleischmann. Joyce began the "Nausicaa" episode a few months later – and wrote it in the flowery, simpering style common to the romantic magazines and novels which Martha read all day. Nora Barnacle never knew about the candlelight relationship and if in fact Joyce succeeded with Martha it is one of the very few, perhaps two, occasions in his life when he was unfaithful to Nora.

Curiously – bearing the mood of "Nausicaa" in mind – the organ of the body it represents is the eye. The nose is included too, but the eye dominates.

> And while she gazed her heart went pitapat. Yes, it was her he was looking at and there was meaning in his look. His eyes burned into her as though they would search her through and through, read her very soul. Wonderful eyes they were, superbly expressive, but could you trust them? She could see at once by his dark eyes and his pale intellectual face that he was a foreigner, the image of the photo she had of Martin Harvey, the matinée idol . . .

In all, the presence of Gerty MacDowell in "Nausicaa", up to the time she leaves the area of Mr. Bloom, generates over a hundred references to eyes, pictures, looking, glancing, seeing, viewing, eyeing.

Sandymount Strand is greatly changed since Bloomsday. The footpaths by the sands have been trimmed and gardened; an enormous rubbish dump has been levelled and grassed. Why did Mr. Bloom and Gerty MacDowell meet in the twilight of Sandymount Strand? Was it because of Joyce's concern with his ailing eyes? Or was he simply tempted by Homer's story of Nausicaa, who finds Ulysses lying exhausted, naked shipwrecked? Nausicaa, as sumptuously attractive as any of the immortal goddesses, is preparing for her wedding and goes to the beach with some handmaidens to wash her clothes and when she finds Ulysses lying there gives him a tunic, a cloak, some sweet oil in a golden flask and a new stature.

Certainly Mr. Bloom leaves Sandymount Strand in a different condition from the one in which he arrived there. His physical excesses brought on by watching Gerty have left him exhausted and drained, but her clear though unspoken romantic interest in him has restored him psychologically. He dozes.

Joyce described "Nausicaa" as written "in a namby-pamby jammy marmalady drawersy style with effects of incense, mariolatry, masturbations, stewed cockles, painter's palette, chit-chat, circumlocution, etc., etc."

He wrote back to Dublin, asking his aunt to send him novelettes. He asked too whether there were trees behind the Church in Sandymount, whether they would be visible from the shore, whether there were steps down from Leahy's Terrace and whether she could send him a penny hymnbook.

"Nausicaa" had *Ulysses* banned in the United States. When it was published in the *Little Review*, a civil servant responsible for protecting New York from Vice brought the publishers to court. Intellectual and artistic defences, the thoughts of Freud and Cubists, were produced to confound the allegations of obscenity. But finally it was Gerty MacDowell showing Mr. Bloom her drawers that lost the publishers' case. The two ladies were fined fifty dollars each, were disappointed not to have been jailed as martyrs to freedom. But the fact that the *Little Review* could no longer publish the emerging chapters of *Ulysses* encouraged Sylvia Beach, a young American in Paris, to offer to publish a book. Thus did Gerty MacDowell's drawers get *Ulysses* published in book form.

In Sandymount now the Strand has been foreshortened: you could never hear the hymns in the Star of the Sea church, nor, easily see fireworks over Ballsbridge. "A bat flew. Here. There. Here. Far in the grey a bell chimed. Mr. Bloom with open mouth, his left boot sanded sidways, leaned, breathed."

A clock chimes, a cuckoo clock, cuckoo
for Bloom, cuckoo for Boylan,
cuckoo for Molly, cuckoo, cuckoo . . .

OXEN OF THE SUN

Squared in regular bricks, the National Maternity Hospital stands at the bottom corner of Merrion Square, lit by the evening sun. Behind it, vaguely symbolic, stands a huge gasometer.

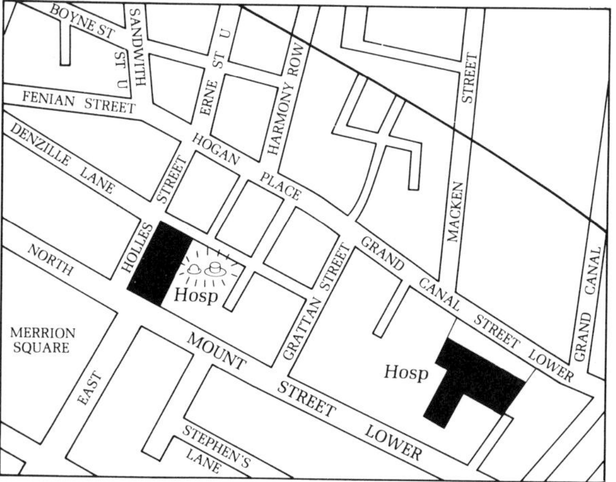

Holles Street Hospital lies along Merion Square, bridging into Lower Mount Street cornering into Holles Street. Merrion Square, on the 16th of June, 1904, was a place of quiet grandeur. It was once a beach, washed by a tide from Ringsend. As a square it was laid out in 1762, elegant and controlled by the Wide Streets Commission. Merrion Square's development spanned the turn of the eighteenth century: it became a place of residence for the gentry and members of the professions.

Their houses were substantial: several, if not all, had mews at the end of the garden for the servants, and these quarters were connected to the main residence by a tunnel or enclosed corridor, mustn't let them blot the landscape. It was a closed, extremely snobbish enclave. People of class and society lived in this encrusted enclave. Dublin was enjoying the beginnings of its great era of medicine, and the physicians who lived in Merrion Square were redoubtable figures, their ladies venturing forth only to visit by carriage or to take the air in the railed enclosure which formed the middle of the square, a locked sward opened only by residents' keys.

The Wildes, Sir William and Speranza, lived at Number One on the same side as the Maternity Hospital. Sheridan Le Fanu drank green tea and wrote his eerie tales at Number Sixty, Merrion Square. In 1904 it was still posh, only slightly bruised by the poverty in the adjacent tenements. It had managed to remain aloft from the squalid city, stayed and secured by its affluence. Once when rebels erupted in a southern county, old men in Merrion Square formed a militia and patrolled their properties in sedan chairs, muskets angled through the curtained windows.

Today the doctors prefer nearby Fitzwilliam Square. The houses and mews of Merrion Square are divided over and over again. Offshoot government departments, dairy produce bodies, solicitors, barristers, controllers of the betting laws, consultant engineers, have purchased corners of corners in these old high houses. Sometimes the subdivision is so obvious: in an office the exquisite frieze will be abruptly bisected by a wooden partition. Ceilings never

SIR
WILLIAM

complete their expanse. Hallways have suffered most: if you stand in a beautiful small antechamber to a huge hallway and as the shining mahogany and brassed door swings back – you are greeted by plywood and glass. A few brave people of taste have taken high apartments and have restored ceilings, panels, plasterwork. For their efforts – a residential bonus.

For generations, the centre of the square had been designated as a site for a Catholic cathedral. Successive Archbishops of Dublin had retained exclusive access – the square was closed, no constitutional walks could be taken without ecclesiastical permission. Now – *nihil obstat*: a new Archbishop elevated the square into a park, squared by embassies, by the National Gallery of Ireland, rich from Shaw, bequeathed by *My Fair Lady*, and by Government Buildings.

> Now let us speak of that fellowship that was there to the intent to be drunken an they might. There was a sort of scholars along either side the board, that is to wit, Dixon yclept junior of saint Mary Merciable's with other his fellows Lynch and Madden, scholars of medicine, and the franklin that hight Lenehan and one from Alba Longa, one Crotthers, and young Stephen that had mien of a frere that was at head of the board and Costello that men clepen Punch Costello all long of a mastery of him erstwhile gested (and all of them, reserved young Stephen, he was the most drunken that demanded still of more mead) and beside the meek Sir Leopold. But on young Malachi they waited for that he promised to have come and such as intended to no goodness said how he had broke his avow. And Sir Leopold sat with them for he bore fast friendship to Sir Simon and to this his son young Stephen and for that his langour becalmed him there after longest wanderings . . .

NATIONAL GALLERY OF IRELAND

"Oxen of the Sun" is the episode in which Mr. Bloom and Stephen meet. A bunch of medical students, Dixon, Lynch, Madden, the hanger-on Lenehan, a Scot called Crotthers, Stephen Dedalus and Punch Costello have been sitting in an anteroom of the maternity hospital waiting for Buck Mulligan to appear, when Mr. Bloom slips in and sits next to drunken Stephen. It is ten o'clock at night and Mr. Bloom enquires into the health of Mrs. Purefoy who is in labour and having a bad time.

Joyce took her name from that of the leading obstetrician of the day in Dublin, Dr. R. Damon Purefoy, and the Christian postnatal ritual of "churching" a woman is intended to purify after birth. The proprietor of the maternity hospital is Sir Andrew Horne: a bull forms a substantial topic of conversation but Joyce's joke is sexual rather than agricultural.

"Oxen of the Sun" is the most complex chapter in *Ulysses*. It took Joyce, by his own reckoning, a thousand hours to write. He designed it in nine segments – to correspond with pregnancy – and while he was working on it he kept before him an onion-shaped diagram to which he crayoned monthly the growth of the embryo. The episode is a literary parody of most of the major writers, Shakespeare excepted, from Mandeville, Swift, Sterne and Dickens, with a loud blast of slang, jargon and pidgin English at the end.

The students and their associates are sitting around discussing birth, sex and women in an extremely coarse fashion. They range over contraception, bestial sexual activity, congress and conquests, and the old dilemma of whom do you save, mother or child, in a difficult birth? Reasoned, quiet Mr. Bloom attempts to defuse: "laying hand to jaw, he said dissembling, as his wont was, that as it was informed him, who had ever loved the art of physic as might a layman, and agreeing also with his experience of so seldom seen an accident". The argument rises until: "Nurse Quigley from the door angerly bid them hist ye should shame you"; as the students are ordered to lower their voices a thunderstorm broke out and electrified Stephen: "and he that had erst challenged to be so doughty waxed pale". Joyce was terrified of lightning.

Lenehan refers to Mr. Deasy's letter about foot-and-mouth disease and cattle. Stephen has arranged publication in the evening paper.

The bull is proffered as a symbol of all that is dominant, male and mythological. "Our worthy acquaintance, Mr. Malachi Mulligan", now appeared in the doorway, accompanied with a friend, Alec Bannon, who has been attempting his luck with Mr. Bloom's daughter Milly in Mullingar. Mulligan amuses everyone vastly and bawdily.

Miss Callan, a nursing sister, arrives to tell Dixon he is required in the ward; Mina Purefoy, to great relief, has given birth to a bouncing boy, her ninth. After more bawdry, melancholy from Mr. Bloom, a sudden appearance by Haines the Englishman, more pouring from bottles, they all leave to drink in a nearby pub called Burke's. J. Burke, publican, licensed his premises at 17, Holles Street. No more, no more, the medicals to-day drink at more suitably-named Ulyssean places.

Even though George Bernard Shaw never finished reading Ulysses he was particularly struck by "Oxen of the Sun". He believed it conveyed such an accurate picture of the foul-mouthed young Dublin rakes, the notorious "medicals", that he wanted to form clubs of them for the sole purpose of making them read *Ulysses*, dare they continue to live, he opined, without reforming profoundly and extensively.

Joyce found the episode the most difficult part of the novel. Ulysses' appeal to his fellow travellers not to destroy the legendary cattle of the sun was a parallel along which Joyce could, he felt, outline the medical students' disrespect for fertility for the women labouring upstairs. Ulysses alone took no part in the slaughter of the oxen, Bloom never contributed to the coarse student exchanges. Ulysses groaned aloud when he came upon the wanton slaughter: Bloom wished inwardly that the young men didn't drink quite so heavily and showed more respect for their patients.

While he was constructing it, Joyce told a friend that he wanted the chapter to convey a crime against fecundity; the students discuss the valuable fruitlessness of contraception. The organ he wished to represent is the womb, medicine the chosen art, white the colour and embryonic

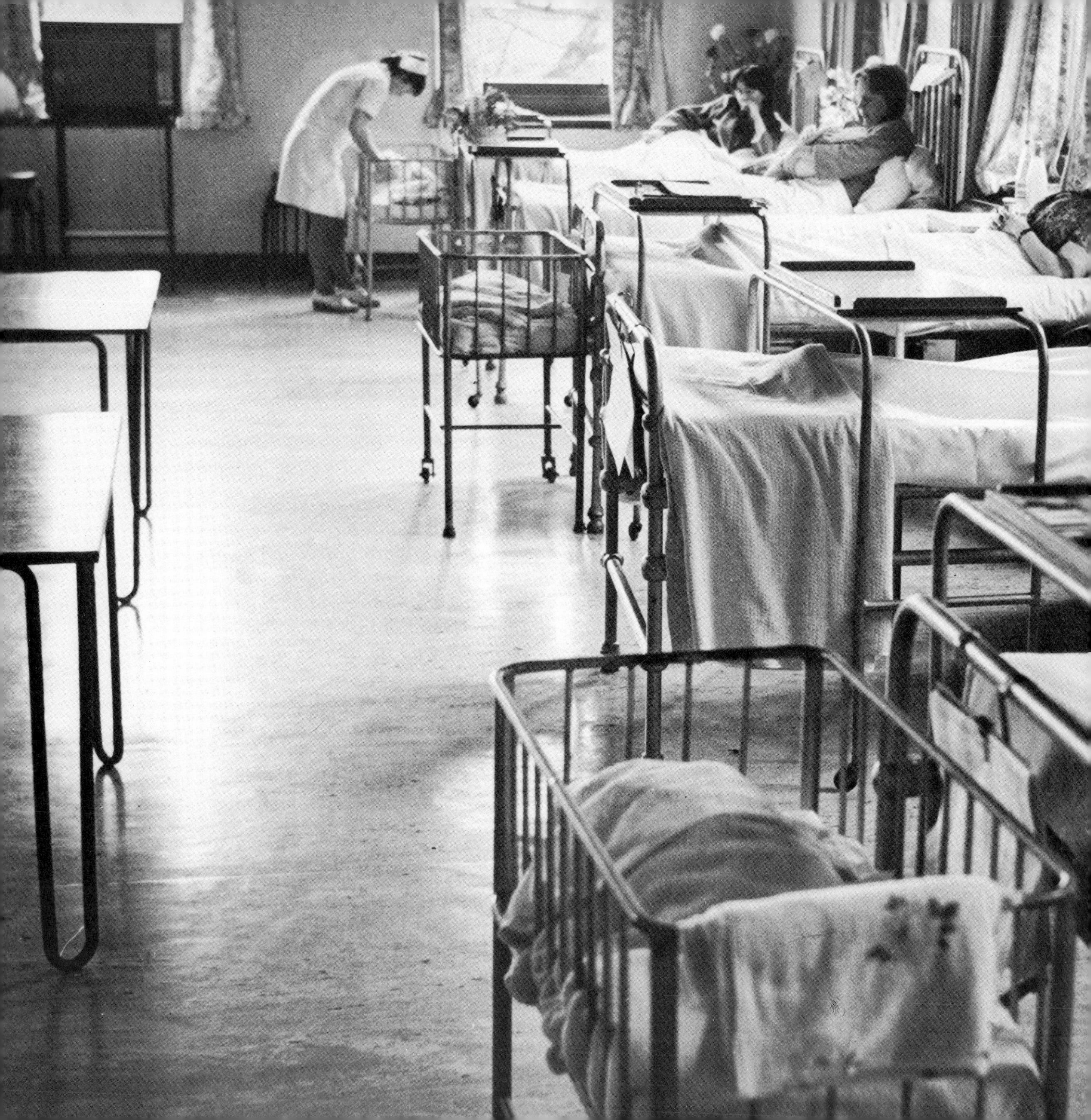

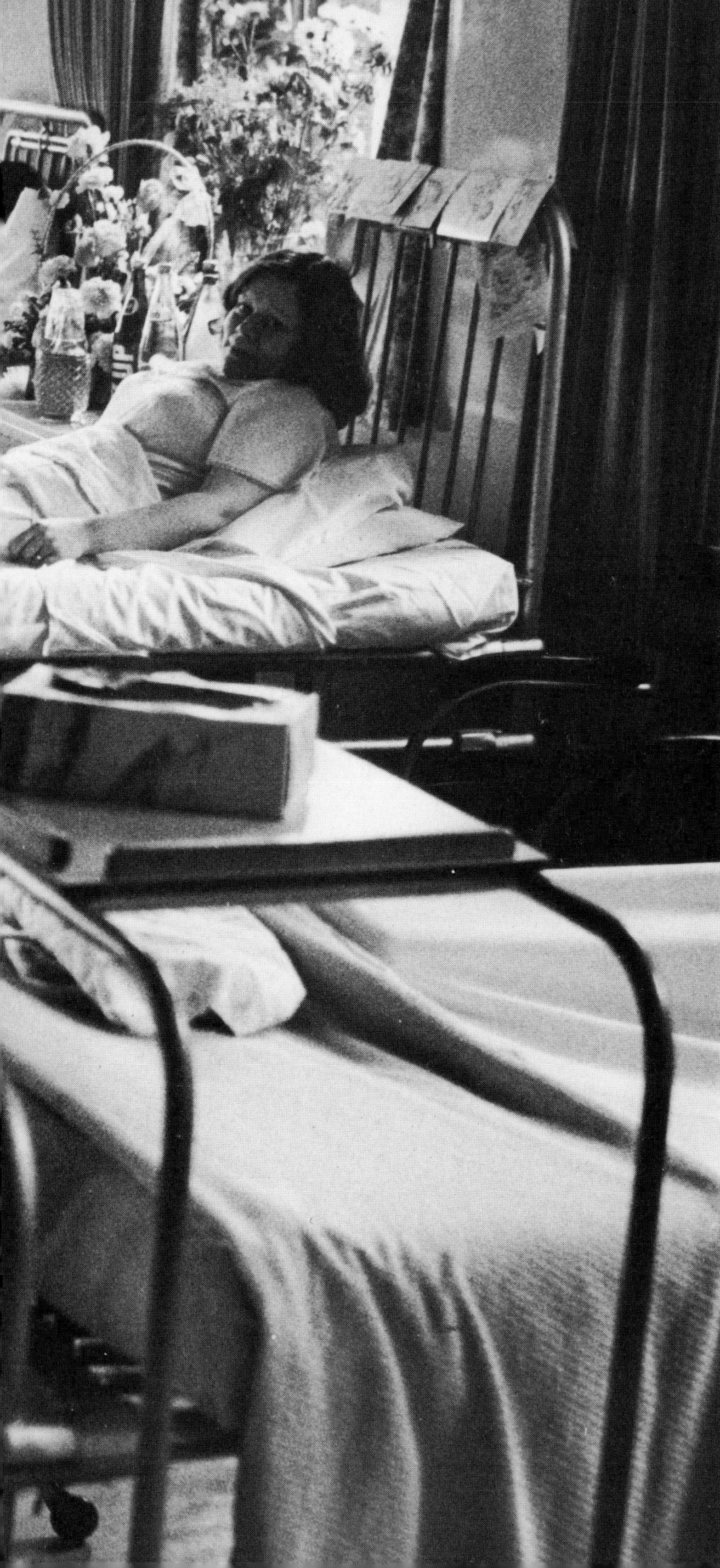

development the technique. He became so involved with the Homeric theme that he felt he himself had eaten oxen, and for months he couldn't sit down to a meal without feeling nauseous.

First he tickled her, then he patted her
Then he passed the female catheter

Dr. Oliver St. John Gogarty, the Buck Mulligan, epitomised the rakish medical student about Dublin. When a colleague who had made a fortune through his renowned surgery lost it all in the divorce that followed a sexual indiscretion, Gogarty described him as "the only man I ever knew who made a fortune with his knife and lost it with his fork". The National Maternity Hospital is no longer the noisome unhygienic building of Bloomsday. And it is involved in an activity which would have appealed to Joyce's symbolic mind. Umbilical cords are gathered, adjusted and converted into bypass transplants for varicose veins.

"The Oxen of the Sun" episode is the most difficult to read in *Ulysses* All Joyce's linguistic interests are on exhibition and he gives a foretaste of what was to come in *Finnegans Wake*. That it exhausted him is certain: in several communications with friends he referred to "the Oxen of the bloody, bleeding Sun" and he admitted freely that the control of all the ideas, the mathematical nine-part divisions, the embryonic developments and the endless parodies were almost as much as he could master. He managed brilliantly.

Pubwards, Mr. Bloom leaves the hospital where Mina Purefoy is relaxing in the hands of "Doctor Diet and Doctor Quiet". After closing time Mr. Bloom and Stephen Dedalus "will seek the kips where shady Mari is. Righto, any old time".

CIRCE

Nighttown that crawling, hag-haunted, gaseous sump, is now derelict. This was the red-light district of gaslit, foggy streets where sin, wild laughter and nightmares were private property.

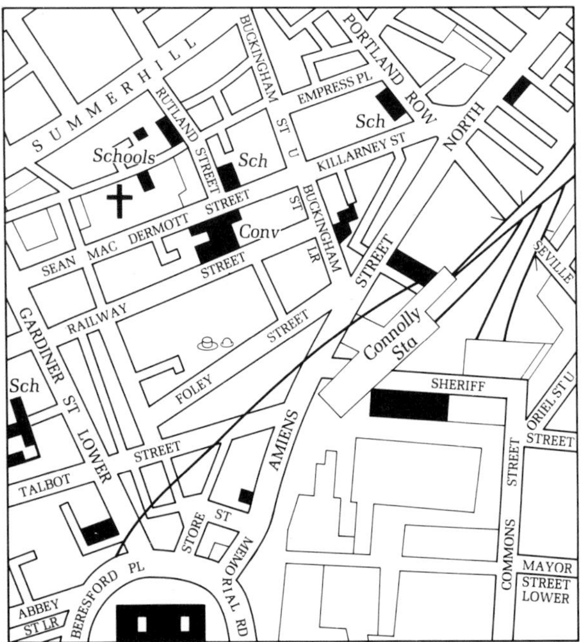

Montgomery Street, "Monto", was Nighttown. So was Corporation Street, Railway Street and Foley Street, all radiating off Talbot Street. Officers, gentlemen and soldiers spent many thirds of their lives there in circumstances as unhygienic as they were bawdy. Montgomery Street, it was agreed, was then the worst slum in Western Europe. In the area between Monto and O'Connell Street two thousand prostitutes urged trade.

The heyday of Nighttown began in the middle of the nineteenth century when a fashionable group of streets gave way to two regiments and their retinue. Nighttown gained Dublin a reputation for unlimited bawdry.

The women flocked to do business in the creaking streets, "those crowds of young girls who take possession of the city when darkness comes and whose demeanour by no means suggests the modesty and decorum we are wont to regard as inseparable from the Irish maiden", was how an eminent Jesuit of the day worried about them.

Some of the women passed into immediate legend. There was Becky Cooper who loved her work so much that she plied enjoyable young men with gifts – and with economic gestures:

Italy's maids are fair to see
And France's maids are willing
But less expensive 'tis to me:
Becky's for a shilling.

Julia Hooligan, engrossed in conversation with a friend in Grafton Street one day, was unwittingly barring the path of a well-known lawyer. "Out of my way, woman," he throated. "And who do you think you are?" Julia nipped back. "Madam – I am the most famous Crown solicitor from here to Balbriggan." "That's nuthin'," chuckled the undaunted Julia. "I'm the most famous *half*-crown solicitor from here to Belfast." Another, Mrs Mack, is alleged to have been visited by the Prince of Wales.

The Prince of Wales lost more than virtue in Dublin. As King Edward the Seventh he later came to the city for an investiture, but the insignia of the Knights of the Order of

Saint Patrick were mysteriously stolen from Dublin Castle days before and consequently no investiture even occurred.

O, there goes Mrs. Mack;
She keeps a house of imprudence,
She keeps an old back parlour
For us poxy medical students.

Mrs. Mack's bedroom had a large washstand containing two jugs in bright yellow basins, a large bed hammocked with age, a sewing-machine, spools of silk, slippers, cigarettes, greasy curl-papers, empty cigarette tins, and on the mantelpiece mottled with cigarette burns were several rancid tumblers and a photograph of a smart trapful of girls. Mrs. Mack's face – Gogarty's description – was brick red "on which avarice was written like a hieroglyphic, and a laugh like a guffaw in hell". Mrs. Mack's parlour was inhabited by a pianist who sat with his face turned to the wall in front of a cottage piano on which stood a half-empty measure of stout.

Florry Talbot's father was asked by the priests why he wouldn't do something about his daughter's disgraceful way of life. "Well," he said thoughtfully and agreeably, "the girl appears to be enjoying herself and besides, well – she's a source of income to me."

Piano Mary dwelt:

Where Hell's gates leave the street,
And all the tunes she used to play
Along your spine beneath the sheet?
She was a morsel passing sweet
And warmer than the gates of Hell.

There was May Oblong and fresh Nellie and Lady Betty and Mrs. Lawless. Some had their own houses full of religious pictures behind which they hid coshes of lead piping in case of trouble. Some worked the Hay Hotel; the windowsills and lower windows were packed with hay to comfort the waiting horses of the visiting gentlemen.

Some became immortal through literature, like the lady at Number Eighty-Two, Railway Street, then Mecklenburgh Street. Here lived Bella Cohen the Circe who lured Mr. Bloom. Her chandelier was covered with mauve tissue paper, an oilcloth on the floor had patterns and colours in mosaics of jade and azure and cinnabar rhomboids. The walls were hung with paper of yew fronds and clear glades and a screen of peacock feathers filled the grate while Bella Cohen sang endlessly.

(The Mabbot Street entrance of Nighttown, before which stretches an uncobbled tramsiding set with skeleton tracks, red and green will-o'-the-wisps and danger signals. Rows of flimsy houses with gaping doors. Rare lamps with faint rainbow fans. Round Rabaiotti's halted ice gondola stunted men and women squabble. They grab wafers between which are wedged lumps of coal and copper snow. Sucking, they scatter slowly. Children. The swancomb of the gondola, highreared, forges on through the murk, white and blue under a lighthouse. Whistles call and answer.)

THE CALLS : Wait, my love, and I'll be with you.
THE ANSWERS : Round behind the stable.

Mr. Bloom leaves the pub loses his way, jumps into a first class carriage by mistake, goes a station too far. He is concerned about the very drunken Stephen, realises that the students are bound for the brothels.

"Circe" is fantasy merging slowly and cruelly into fact. The longest chapter in the entire novel, it is a psychedelic hallucination, fantastic nightmare, written as dramatic performance with actions,

characterisations and descriptions embodied in the "stage directions" – reactions, imaginations and subconscious fears in the verbal exchanges. All sorts of echoes ring out – for Macbeth's three witches Joyce has Kitty, Zoe and Florry; Gerty MacDowell, Cissy Caffrey and Edy Boardman appear bawdily transmuted from the sweet-smelling moments on Sandymount Strand; Paddy Dignam returns from the grave: "Half of one ear, all the nose and thumbs are ghouleaten." Mrs. Breen, J. J. O'Molloy. Tom Rochford, Bob Doran, Myles Crawford, several of the minor characters from previous chapters reappear – and a few others, Edward VII, Shakespeare and Alfred Lord Tennyson; Philip Drunk and Philip Sober, two Oxford dons – they are Siamese twins with lawnmowers.

Mr. Bloom undergoes a mock trial for interfering with Mary Driscoll, a housemaid: his ancestors offer advice, his wife abuse, and finally he succumbs to the longed-for violence of Bella Cohen.

> (*The door opens. Bella Cohen, a massive whoremistress enters. She is dressed in a three-quarter ivory gown, fringed round the hem with tasselled selvedge, and cools herself, flirting a black horn fan like Minni Hauck in* Carmen. *On her left hand are wedding and keeper rings. Her eyes are deeply carboned. She has a sprouting moustache. Her olive face is heavy, slightly sweated and fullnosed, with orange-tainted nostrils. She has large pendant beryl eardrops*).
> BELLA : My word! I'm all of a mucksweat.
> (*She glances around her at the couples. Then her eyes rest on Bloom with hard insistence. Her large fan winnows wind towards her heated face, neck and embonpoint. Her falcon eyes glitter.*)
> THE FAN : (*flirting quickly, then slowly*) Married, I see.

And from then on Mr. Bloom gets who-began-it, vile abuse, to his great delight, even being obliged to lace Bella's boot.

The fan is not the only inanimate object with a speaking part. Yew trees, Sleepy Hollow, Halcyon Days, an Echo, a Dummy, a Waterfall, a Pianola, a Gasjet, a Horse, a Retriever, Brass Quoits, and assorted nymphs, hobgoblins and bracelets clamour and clang in a long, mad, luminous, swirling saraband of images that fog and fill your mind and drag you along in a crazy punk rag-doll, dervish, dance.

> *(Gazelles are leaping, feeding on the mountains. Near are lakes. Round their shores file shadows black of cedargroves. Aroma rises, a strong hairgrowth of resin. It burns, the orient, a sky of sapphire, cleft by the bronze flight of eagles. Under it lies the womancity, nude, white, still, cool, in luxury. A fountain murmurs among damask roses. Mammoth roses murmur of scarlet winegrapes. A wine of shame, lust, blood exudes, strangely murmuring.)*

There is a young fellow named Joyce
Who possesses a sweet tenor voice.
He goes down to the kips,
With a psalm on his lips,
And biddeth the harlots rejoice.
Oliver St. J. Gogarty

Joyce's first sexual experience was with a prostitute on a canal bank when he was fourteen. Subsequently in Nighttown and in Paris he paid them frequent visits and got, as well as such sexual gratification as he sought, the Irish thrill of religious guilt. At the time of that first vivid canalbank moment he was an active member of the sodality of the Blessed Virgin Mary in School: thereafter all

carnal knowledge was tinged with guilt and shame in some way. When his relationship with Nora filled out, his wanderings largely ceased. He did record to friends his encounter with Martha Fleischmann, the lame girl who was the prototype for Gerty MacDowell. After his "sojourn" with Martha on the night of his thirty-seventh birthday, Candlemas Day, the 2nd of February, 1919, he told a friend that he had "explored the hottest and coldest parts of a woman's body".

The bulk of the action in "Circe" takes place, appropriately, around midnight. Stephen shows up, is knocked down brutally in a confrontation between two foul-mouthed soldiers to whom Joyce gave the names of two British civil servants he had argued with in Zurich. The widening circles which Mr. Bloom and Stephen have described about each other all day, around the book-barrows, around the National Library, along Sandymount Strand, close inwards when Mr. Bloom takes charge of Stephen who is too bruised, too shocked and too drunk to take care of himself. Endless references in "Circe" to the Mass, Stephen a sacrificial victim, a Christ figure, blood and wine, all set Ireland's teeth on edge against Joyce.

The motor parts of the body, the endless need to move, were the physiological parallels. Magic glitters, religious, literary, scientific, artistic, linguistic, topographical, social, political magic. When he had written "Circe" and re-written it up to nine times, Joyce allowed himself a rare compliment by asserting his belief that it was perhaps "the best thing he had ever done".

May Oblong's gone and Mrs. Mack,
Fresh Nellie's gone and Number Five
Where you could get so good a back
And drinks were so superlative.
Of all their nights, oh man alive!
There is not left an oyster shell
Where greens are gone the grays will thrive;
There's only left the Hay Hotel.

The Gogarty lament became redundant in 1925 when a preaching priest dared suggest that such

ERRUM TRADING

an unsavoury place existed in Dublin. And on the 12th of March, in the middle of Lent, Catholic vigilantes, supported by the police, went in like an army. That well-known Irish disease, "Scuffles", broke out; whores were arrested, so were citizens and visitors, including a member of the Irish Parliament who protested until he was red in the face (which he was anyway) that he was only in there for a drink. The Legion of Mary, a white army which still marches under the banner of the Mother of God, was the conqueror: when the back-up force of Legion ladies rosaried through the area within days the saddened, remaining, redundant whores knelt in the streets, and watched the silent, compassionate, benign conquerors pin holy pictures on the brothel doors.

No such area as Nighttown exists in Dublin now. Prostitution is no longer a "problem". When Gogarty became a senator the trees on the canal bank, under which the descendants of fresh Nellie, Mrs. Mack, and Piano Mary entertained their clients, were threatened by zealous politicians. Gogarty pleaded for the trees, argued that they were "more sinned against than sinning". As Mr. Bloom leaves Nighttown, he has a vision.

> *(Against the dark wall a figure appears slowly, a fairy boy of eleven, a changeling, kidnapped, dressed in an Eton suit with glass shoes and a little bronze helmet, holding a book in his hand. He reads from right to left inaudibly, smiling, kissing the page.)*
> BLOOM: *(Wonderstruck, calls inaudibly)* Rudy!

If his baby son Rudy had lived he would be eleven. Bloom, in fact, with Stephen, and in fantasy with Rudy, has found his son. His odyssey is coming to a long, slow, thoughtful, curling conclusion.

EUMAEUS

The sadness, the dark, in Dublin late at night is swingeing. People who do not want to go home, who will not go home, who have not got a home, lurch and stagger in the gloom, moths without a candle.

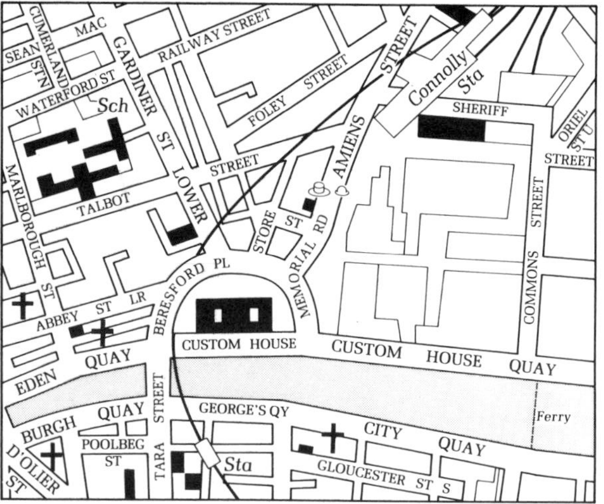

When Mr. Bloom left Nighttown, Stephen Dedalus in tow, he turned into Amiens Street, sought a cab – in vain – and steered a course for Butt Bridge. Ahead, the Custom House; to the left of Mr. Bloom, then as now, the Italianate pile of Amiens Street railway station from which you may bear north through Balbriggan and Drogheda and Dundalk to Belfast, an old, historic journey. Here, in easier times, the Thursday shopping excursions departed for Belfast: here returned the Contraceptive Express, a train of women testing the laws which forbade the sale of, the use of. A canvassed government whig, stoutly, Catholicly, insisted against contraceptives. "But I wouldn't mind using a French letter."

"Preparatory to anything else Mr. Bloom brushed off the greater bulk of the shavings and handed Stephen the hat and ashplant and bucked him up generally in orthodox Samaritan fashion, which he very badly needed." Stephen has had an altercation with a couple of private soldiers at the entrance to Nighttown and is none the better for it. He is dusted down by Mr. Bloom, as James Joyce was once dusted down by that Jewish good Samaritan, Alfred Hunter.

Stephen has a drink in mind and Mr. Bloom imagined the possibilities of perhaps a glass of milk or a mineral or even some pure water from the River Vartry, reservoired into Dublin. The cabman's shelter at Butt Bridge will provide the necessary facilities. Getting there – Stephen is intoxicated and Mr. Bloom is tired – makes walking a weary hazard.

It is after midnight.

They passed the main entrance of the Great Northern Railway Station, the starting point for Belfast, where of course all traffic was suspended at that late hour, and, passing the back door of the morgue (a not very enticing locality, not to say gruesome to a degree, more especially at night), ultimately gained the Dock Tavern and in due course turned into Store Street, famous for its C division police station.

Today, Store Street is still a busy police station. A building has been added, Bus Áras, the house of the omnibus: from here towns are connected to Dublin like a childrens' puzzle which joins the numbered dots. This clanging building was unwrapped in 1953, the first postwar attempt at modern Irish architecture, a gallant try. Slowly, with tired certainty, "they made a beeline across the back of the Customhouse and passed under the Loop Line bridge when a brazier of coke burning in front of a sentrybox, or something like one, attracted their rather lagging footsteps".

Somniferously, James Joyce is winding down his long odyssey. Stephen and Mr. Bloom have met. Telemachus has met his father Ulysses, the young man has met the older Everyman, youth and maturity are in each other's arms.

Mr. Bloom is concerned about Stephen, even advises him that going down to the kips, to be Gogartian about it, was not a good idea,

> spoke a word of caution *re* the dangers of Nighttown, women of ill fame and swell mobsmen, which, barely permissible once in a while, though not as a habitual practice, was of the nature of a regular deathtrap for young fellows of his age particularly if they had acquired drinking habits under the influence of liquor unless you knew a little jujitsu for every contingency as even a fellow on the broad of his back could administer a nasty kick if you didn't look out.

Mr. Bloom, tired man, is beginning to drone a little; young Dedalus, on home-made wings, is flying above, a little ahead, far enough away for earshot to be unimportant. Joyce controlled most of his male relationships in such a fashion. He was the acceptor, rarely the initiator. Only where there was blood relationship did he show his colours.

The three significant male relatives were his father John, his brother Stanislaus, his son Giorgio. His father died in Dublin in 1931 at the age of eighty-two, Stanislaus died in Trieste on the 16th of June, 1955, at the age of seventy-one, Giorgio was born in July 1905. Joyce and Nora had one other child, Lucia. Since 1945 she has lived in England, cared for in a hospice in Northampton, the survivor.

The relationship between John Joyce and his son was loving, lifelong, despite their separation. As a child Joyce was delighted in, encouraged, admired by his father, who took him on business trips – usually to patch a hole in some sinking argosy. He was shrewd enough to know that his son's mind had possibilities, vain enough to boast about him. When *Ulysses* was published in Dublin and the city was reeling under its scatology and its fingerprinting of Dubliners John Joyce, who did not pretend to read or understand it, accepted mystification, smiled at the effects his genius son was having on Dublin: Jim was "a nice sort of blackguard".

The relationship with Stanislaus was a different matter altogether. He was two years and ten months younger than James, he was the third child in the family. His earlier literary ambitions were doomed to shadow. Stanislaus was the more responsible, had a quieter air, a more serious visage. He followed to Trieste, where his role lay halfway between butler and lord chamberlain. He came to the domestic rescue on several occasions, dealt with debt collectors, consoled Nora when times were hard, was often a protesting provider.

He took it upon himself to be his brother's literary critic, unwelcomed by James. He greatly admired *Ulysses*, condemned one or two chapters. For *Finnegans Wake* he employed words like "drivelling rigmarole" and "witless wandering" – James' brain was finally softening. His diary's earlier perceptions of his older brother are revealing.

> He has extraordinary moral courage – courage so great that I have hoped he will one day become the Rousseau of Ireland . . . His manner is generally very engaging and courteous with strangers, but, though he greatly dislikes to be rude, I think there is little courtesy in his nature . . . As he sits on the hearthrug, his arms embracing his knees, his head thrown a little back, his hair brushed up straight off his forehead, his long face red as an Indian's in the reflexion of the fire, there is a look of cruelty on his face . . . Jim is a genius of character . . . But few people will love him in spite of his graces and his genius and whosoever exchanges kindnesses with him is likely to get the worst of the bargain . . .

Stanislaus was always jealous of James' attentiveness to surrounding friends and acquaintances. From University days this jealousy persisted: he loathed Gogarty, for example, whom he described as like Punch, hooked nose and chin to match. Gogarty, ineffably true to form, had written a cruel poem about Stanislaus (Gogarty's nickname for Joyce was Kinch – the word "felt like a blade"):

Poet Kinch has a brother called Thug
His imitator, and jackal, and mug.
His stride like a lord's is
His pretension absurd is
In fact he's an *awful* thick-lug.

Stanislaus Joyce was a good, kind man who was never wanded with his brother's magic. But oh! How he wished to be!

Giorgio Joyce sang like an angel and swam like an athlete. He was tall and handsome like his father, brushed with some of his mother's good looks. He was agreeably fiery, wasn't easily pushed about by his father. Giorgio received the exaggerated affectionate courtesy which Joyce bestowed quietly upon his children.

"Stephen of his own accord stopped for no special reason to look at the heap of barren cobblestones and by the light emanating from the brazier he could just make out the darker figure of the corporation watchman inside the gloom of the sentrybox." Eumaeus, the swineherd, sits in a little hut and discourses in the direction of Ulysses, who is reunited with Telemachus in front of the hut. "Mr. Bloom in the meanwhile kept dodging about in the vicinity of the cobblestones near the brazier of coke in front of the corporation watchman's sentrybox, who, evidently a glutton for work, it struck him, was having a quiet forty winks for all intents and purposes on his own private account while Dublin slept." The "Eumaeus" episode of *Ulysses* represents the nervous system: Stephen is under the influence of drink, Mr. Bloom is under the influence of Stephen and wishes to see to him, feed and rest him. Excised from Mulligan and Haines where will Stephen stay? "I don't mean to presume to dictate to you in the slightest degree but why did you leave your father's house? To seek misfortune, was Stephen's answer". Both men lurch easily to the cabmen's shelter at Butt Bridge.

Night in Dublin makes the city dark and old and Victorian and Edwardian. Gaslight would not be too surprising: Dublin is a nightcity. Isolated forgotten tramps phantom the pavements, police patrol in cars or pairs. A few open cafés gather in the drifters, the jilted, the jetsam, as a pound rounds up strays.

"Mr. Bloom and Stephen entered the cabman's shelter, an unpretentious wooden structure, where, prior to then, he had rarely, if ever, been before"; and to where they have now come in

search of a night's collation. It has disappeared now, this anteroom to Purgatory, flotsammed with a "decidedly miscellaneous collection of waifs and strays and other nondescript specimens of the genus *homo*". Mr. Bloom and his new-found friend – who, by dint of his writing and musical abilities may yet assist Mr. Bloom's suddenly budding impresario ambitions – attempt sustenance. An able seaman, one W. B. Murphy, addresses them, tells tall stories. This sailor came up the river at eleven o'clock in the morning. He was on board that high ship Stephen saw, from Sandymount Strand "the threemaster *Rosevean* from Bridgwater with bricks". There is much conversation between the able seaman and the assembled company, which includes the notorious proprietor Skin-the-Goat, a man who has been involved in dark deeds. The sailor displays his chest tattoo, a face named Antonio, who may be made to smile by the manipulation of the flesh.

Mr. Bloom, however, displays a photograph of his wife:

> a large sized lady, with her fleshy charms on evidence in an open fashion, as she was in the full bloom of womanhood, in evening dress cut ostentatiously low for the occasion to give a liberal display of bosom, with more than vision of breasts, her full lips parted, and some perfect teeth, standing near, ostensibly with gravity, a piano . . .

O, it is late and Mr. Bloom is tired, his mind wanders. He picks up a newspaper which contains the report of poor Dignam's death, of the Throwaway victory in the Gold Cup. Coffee bad, conversation not much better: Joyce's style is deliberately tabloid. He draws Stephen away from the cabmen's shelter where the talk is of Parnell, the lost leader.

What has come together now? In the newspaper poor Dignam's funeral, the Gold Cup, the foot-and-mouth letter from Mr. Deasy, the threemaster *Rosevean* from Bridgwater. Mr. Joyce is drawing all the strings together, plucks the last notes from them. There is yet a reprise to come, Mr. Joyce will not let the orchestra go home without a last long note. At a friend's house in Switzerland late one night Joyce and Giorgio sang sweet sad songs for their host. He begged them to stay. Joyce, smiling, spoke a gracious "No". Mr. Bloom, too, must go home.

ITHACA

Number Seven, Eccles Street is closed down now. But it is not dead. In here somewhere, in the grass and the weeds and the masticated rubble, lie the pieces of Mr. Bloom's day. His life and his wife are open to the sky above, and the wind, and Dublin's night.

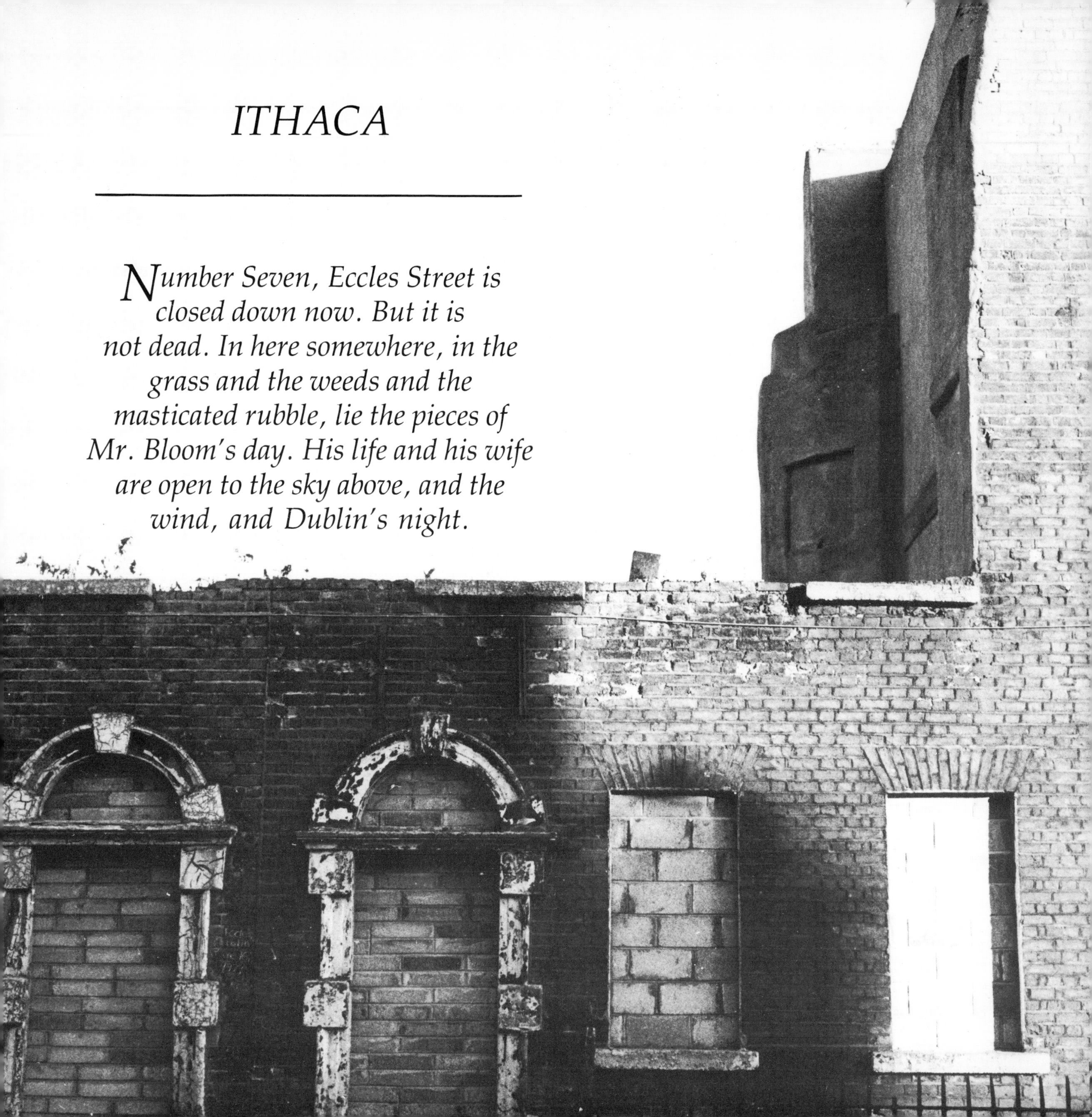

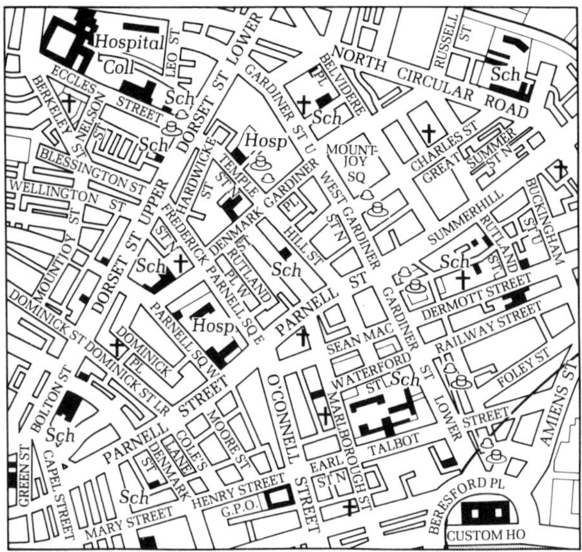

What parallel courses did Bloom and Stephen follow returning?

Starting united both at normal walking pace from Beresford Place they followed in the order named Lower and Middle Gardiner streets and Mountjoy square, west: then, at reduced pace, each bearing left, Gardiner's place by an inadvertence as far as the farther corner of Temple street, north: then at reduced pace with interruptions of halt, bearing right, Temple street, north, as far as Hardwicke place. Approaching, disparate, at relaxed walking pace they crossed both the circus before George's church diametrically, the chord in any circle being less than the arc which it subtends.

Mr. Bloom is home, the Wanderer has returned, Ulysses has come back to Ithaca bringing Telemachus, his son, with him. Murmuring, singing snatches of song, Mr. Bloom and Stephen Dedalus have wound a slow, friendly way home, meshed simply, loosely, inconsequentially in tiredness, inebriation, feeble thought. Music, medicine, the world at large, women – topics which come out at night. It is one o'clock in the morning of the 17th of June, 1904, it is still Bloomsday in lonely Dublin. Mr. Bloom has taken Stephen fully under his wing; kindness and respect for learning.

What action did Bloom make on their arrival at their destination?

At the housesteps of the 4th of the equidifferent uneven numbers, number 7 Eccles Street, he inserted his hand mechanically into the back pocket of his trousers to obtain his latchkey.

Joyce described the style of "Ithaca". the penultimate chapter in *Ulysses*, as the form of a mathematical catechism. Every passage either begins with a question or a statement.

"Was it there? It was in the corresponding pocket of the trousers which he had worn on the day but one preceding."

Mr. Bloom lowers himself into the basement area and drops gently into the space beside the door.

Did he fall?

By his body's known weight of eleven stone and four pounds in avoirdupois measure, as certified by the graduated machine for periodical selfweighing in the premises of Francis Froedman, pharmaceutical chemist of Nineteen, Frederick Street, North, on the last feast of the Ascension, to wit, the twelfth day of May of the bissextile year one thousand nine hundred and four of the christian era (jewish era five thousand six hundred and sixtyfour, mohammedan era one thousand three hundred and twentytwo), golden number five, epact thirteen, solar cycle nine, dominical letters C.B. Roman indication two, Julian period 6617, MXMIV.

Whew! And the entire chapter displays the same knowledge. Everything is grist to the Joycean mill. Mr. Bloom turns on a tap – there is a detailed account of the flowing water in the Roundwood reservoir to Number Seven, Eccles Street. Mr. Bloom's budget for the day occasions a detailed, furnished account of the kind of property an affluent Mr. Bloom would purchase.

"Ithaca" is James Joyce in the highest of high spirits. ". . . Wonderworker, the world's greatest remedy for rectal complaints direct from Wonderworker." Wonderworker is the suppository which apparently "assists nature in the most formidable way" both in men and in ladies who "find Wonderworker especially useful, a pleasant surprise when they note delightful result like a cool drink of fresh spring water on a sultry summer's day". Wonderworker has numerous testimonials, too

from clergyman, British naval officer, well-known author, city man, hospital nurse, lady, mother of five, absentminded beggar.

How did absentminded beggar's concluding testimonial conclude?

What a pity the government did not supply our men with wonderworkers during the South African campaign! What a relief it would have been!

Who, or what, or which manner of man was James A. Joyce? He was born on the 2nd of February, 1882 at Number Forty-One, Brighton Square West in Rathgar. Already his epiphenomena had begun: Brighton Square is not a square, but a triangle! He died in Zurich on the 13th of January, 1941 and is buried there. He was devoted, in his fashion, to his woman Nora Barnacle and his two children, Giorgio and Lucia. He was a remote man who had difficulty trusting anyone. His chief emotional appetite was a psychological one too: happily for him his birth and membership of the Irish race fed his paranoia. He worked harder than most writers in the world have ever done, noting down, making important the ordinary events of life, making what seems small important, what seems commonplace extraordinary.

He was a thin man, in personality and physique: once when his family were tired from want of food he lay back in desultory exultation and announced that he had retired from public life, such as it was. He borrowed clothes, money and food, for himself, his family and his lifestyle. When money was available he dressed like a dandy, lived like a lord in the best restaurants. He was patronised by wealthy women on whom he unfailingly turned. He never smiled without thinking about it first.

He quarrelled with people outside his domain – outside, that is, his inner world, and that included his family and his writings. His greeting to a fellow writer might as easily have been abusive – as when

he told James Stephens at their first meeting that he (Stephens) didn't know the difference between a colon and a semi-colon; a true Joycean will dart immediately to the cloacal pun which Joyce may or may not have intended and it is that "may or may not" which perennates his fascination. He had little patience with intellectual scroungers and scant respect, in the same vein, for those who built sheds instead of castles – even the effort was not worthy of his consideration. From the earliest adulthood he believed himself to be a genius and he worked hard at proving to himself and to the world that he was. He eschewed vociferously and cholerically the Catholic faith of his upbringing – yet his books are full of religious references, some not at all irreverent or blasphemous, his chief crime in Ireland. He was immensely cutting to people who frightened him – even more so to those who did not. He was impatient of commerce, failed at it several times; his essays into enterprise included an attempt to found the first cinema in Dublin (it folded), to import Irish Tweed into Trieste (it faded). He was a teacher, a tenant, a trial. "A man of small virtue, inclined to alcoholism," he told his doctor.

As an author, his biographer Richard Ellmann summarised him:

> Joyce is the porcupine of authors. His heroes are grudged heroes – the impossible young man, the passive adult, the whisky-drinking greybeard. It is hard to like them, harder to admire them. Joyce prefers it so. Unequivocal sympathy would be romancing. He denudes man of what we are accustomed to respect, then summons us to sympathise. For Joyce, as for Socrates, understanding is a struggle, best when humiliating. We can move closer to him by climbing over the obstacles of our pretensions, but as we do so he tasks our prowess again by his difficult language. He requires that we adapt ourselves in form as well as in content to his new point of view. His heroes are not easy liking, his books are not easy reading. He does not wish to conquer us, but to have us conquer him. There are, in other words, no invitations, but the door is ajar.

Mr. Bloom negotiated safely the drop into the area, opened the door by its latch. Joyce had written home to his aunt to enquire whether a man might safely descend from the railings on the street into the open basement of the house and drop the remaining few feet, as he had once seen his friend Byrne do. Stephen waited on the pavement outside until Mr. Bloom, candlelit, let him through the silent darkened hall door.

The island of Ithaca, south-west of the heel of Italy, north-east of the head of the Peloponnese, below Corfu, was the home of Ulysses. While he was away presumed dead, his faithful wife Penelope wove and waited, beset with suitors. To each one, she made the same answer, that she would choose when she finished her loomful. But every night, to ward off decision, she unravelled all she had woven that day and always had work in progress. And when Ulysses came home, the walls of Ithaca ran red with the blood of the suitors.

Mr. Bloom is aware that there have been suitors to his Penelope during the afternoon – rehearsing "Love's Old Sweet Song", no less. He bids Stephen a good night as the clock on Saint George's Church steeple rings half past one.

Heigho, heigho,
Heigho, heigho.

Where were the several members of the company which with Bloom that day at the bidding of that peal had travelled from Sandymount in the south to Glasnevin in the north?

Martin Cunningham (in bed), Jack Power (in bed), Simon Dedalus (in bed), Tom Kernan (in bed), Ned Lambert (in bed), Joe Hynes (in bed), John Henry Menton (in bed), Bernard Corrigan (in bed), Patsy Dignam (in bed), Paddy Dignam (in the grave).

All Mr Bloom's side of Eccles Street is hollow now. From the Mater Hospital to Dorset Street is a sad facade. Even the Dominican Convent with its little baroque basilica will go the way of all developers flesh. Behind the facade of Mr Bloom's house there are weeds in the rubble. Some of the houses have yet to fall – nearby, by poking into the creaking hallway it is still possible to follow Mr Bloom's footsteps as he returns to his little Ithaca and surrounds himself with his possessions which invaders have touched in his absence. In these rooms dwelt the first of Dublin's twentieth-century petit-bourgeoisie: here among their old calendars and almanacs and milk-bottles they became, in time, a risen people.

Mr. Bloom, thoughts whirling in his mind like planets, enters his front room to find furniture rearranged, presumably by the visiting Boylan. Joyce catalogues the room's contents, furniture, books. It is an ordinary sort of room, easy chairs, rectangular rug, "a sofa upholstered in prune plush", a blue and white majolica-topped table, a piano, "its musicrest supporting the music in the key of G natural for voice and piano of *Love's Old Sweet Song* (words by G. Clifton Bingham, composed by J. L. Molloy, sung by Madam Antoinette Sterling) open at the last page with the final indications *ad libitum, forte,* pedal, *animato,* sustained, pedal, *ritirando,* close".

Mr. Bloom's house was laid out as follows: through the hallway the front room, parlour, living-room, is on the left, behind it the bow-windowed bedroom where Molly sleeps in her brassquoitjingling bed. After a short flight of stairs down to a small landing, a door leads to the back garden and the privy. Continue down the stairs to the kitchen, opening on to the area into which keyforgetting Mr. Bloom has dropped gently and safely.

How did Bloom prepare a collation for a gentile?

He poured into two teacups two level spoonfuls, four in all, of Epp's soluble cocoa and proceeded according to the directions for use printed on the label, to each adding after sufficient time for infusion the prescribed ingredients for diffusion in the manner and quantity prescribed.

Being a kindly and courteous gentleman, Mr. Bloom decides to use, not his own favourite moustache cup of imitation Crown Derby "but a cup identical with that of his guest". He and Stephen sit and drink cocoa, Mr. Bloom drinking somewhat quicker than his young guest. Stephen's jacket is torn, Stephen has refused to wash his stained face and hands, "distrusting aquacities". Such firm eccentricity in one so learned makes Mr. Bloom think of poetry and literature.

An ambition to squint
At my verses in print
Makes me hope that for these you'll find room.
If you so condescend
Then please place at the end
The name of yours truly, L. Bloom.

There were a few families of Bloom in Dublin in Joyce's time. One was a dentist whose son was a dentist. Another Mr. Bloom murdered a girl in some sort of rural death pact. He failed, however, to kill himself and, Manson-like, scrawled the word "LOVE" on the wall, but could not get the spelling right – it emerged as a scarlet, dripping "LIOVE".

The last notes of Blazes Boylan fade away – yesterday's hit parade . . .

Joyce intended "Ithaca" to represent the skeleton. The bones of the day are recorded in Mr. Bloom's budget, from the first kidney in Dlugacz's meat shop, to the coffee and bun in the cabman's shelter. Such financial considerations excite Mr. Bloom's ambitions and he dreams of being a sleek landed gentleman, a man attractive to courtesans, a businessman, a financier, a man apart. Mr. Bloom in his own home at nearly two o'clock in the morning, looking through the drawers of his life and his household, emerges finally as a lovable, harmless, slightly gormless man: mildly crafty, often lonely, gently enquiring, a loner who pays his own ticket, a dreamer of dreams which he is afraid to make come true, a hurt, slightly odd, generous, undriving, wandering thirty-eight-year-old Dublin Jew.

£5 reward lost, stolen or strayed from his residence Seven Eccles Street, missing gent about forty, answering to the name of Bloom, Leopold (Poldy), height 5ft. 9½ inches, full build, olive complexion, may have since grown a beard, when last seen was wearing a black suit. Above sum will be paid for information leading to his discovery.

What universal binomial denominations would be his as entity and nonentity?

Assumed by any or known to none. Everyman or Noman.

Mr. Bloom is alive and well and is going to bed. Mr. Bloom puts on a white nightshirt and climbs into bed beside his wife. "He kissed the plump mellow yellow smellow melons of her rump . . ." and lay with his feet beside her head, his head at the foot of the bed. Not since five weeks before their son Rudy was born have Mr. Bloom and Molly made love. That was ten years, five months and eighteen days before Bloomsday.

Wakened Molly mutters. They lie there in the dim. They are "at rest relatively to themselves and to each other. In motion being each and both carried westward, forward and rereward respectively, by the proper perpetual motion of the earth through everchanging tracks of neverchanging space." The globe spins on and Mr. and Mrs. Bloom, upside down in bed, spin with it.

PENELOPE

Molly Bloom is life itself. When kissed and yielding in Howth, when deep asleep upstairs, she is the end, and the beginning, and the continuation of Bloom's day.

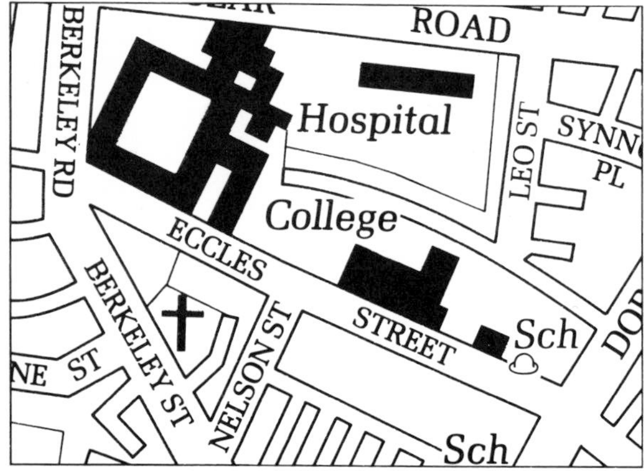

"I can't write," came a letter from Joyce to his brother. "Nora is trying on a pair of drawers by the wardrobe. Excuse me."

"He knows at all nothing about women," said his wife once. He signed ceremonially the first copy of *Ulysses* for Nora and she immediately offered to sell it to a young friend who was there at the time. Later, when they were invited to the ballet to celebrate the 16th of June, she didn't know why the date was significant.

In May 1921 Joyce said that he was completing "Ithaca", a "mathematico-astronomico-physico-mechanico-geometrico-chemico sublimation of Bloom and Stephen (devil take 'em both) to prepare for the final amplitudinously curvilinear episode, 'Penelope'." The first sentence was to contain two and half thousand words, the entire chapter no more than eight sentences, to begin and end with "the most positive word in the English language, the word *yes*". It takes place in Molly's bed-mind, a stream of life flowing through her. ("Yes because he never did a thing like that before as ask to get his breakfast in bed with a couple of eggs . . .") Molly Bloom's soliloquy was regarded as the most obscene chapter in the novel. The monologue interieur, is brought to its highest point in Molly's ramblings across her life, her world in Number Seven, Eccles Street, her husband, her lovers, her prospects.

Joyce was better with women than with men. When he fell in love with Nora, and she with him, he decided to be as true as he could to her. They had a difficult life: he was generally uncaring and hereditarily accustomed to living on his wits, tomorrow would take care of the debt collector. The greater burden of their world fell on Nora. She had come from candid Catholic West of Ireland stock and bravely dashed into exile with a complex man she hardly knew. She adored Joyce without being overawed by him: no matter what pinnacle the world built for him she stayed within reach of herself.

He relished her tartness, her rigid propriety, moral disciplines, her friendliness and hospitality. More than one friend has borne witness that Nora was the one who

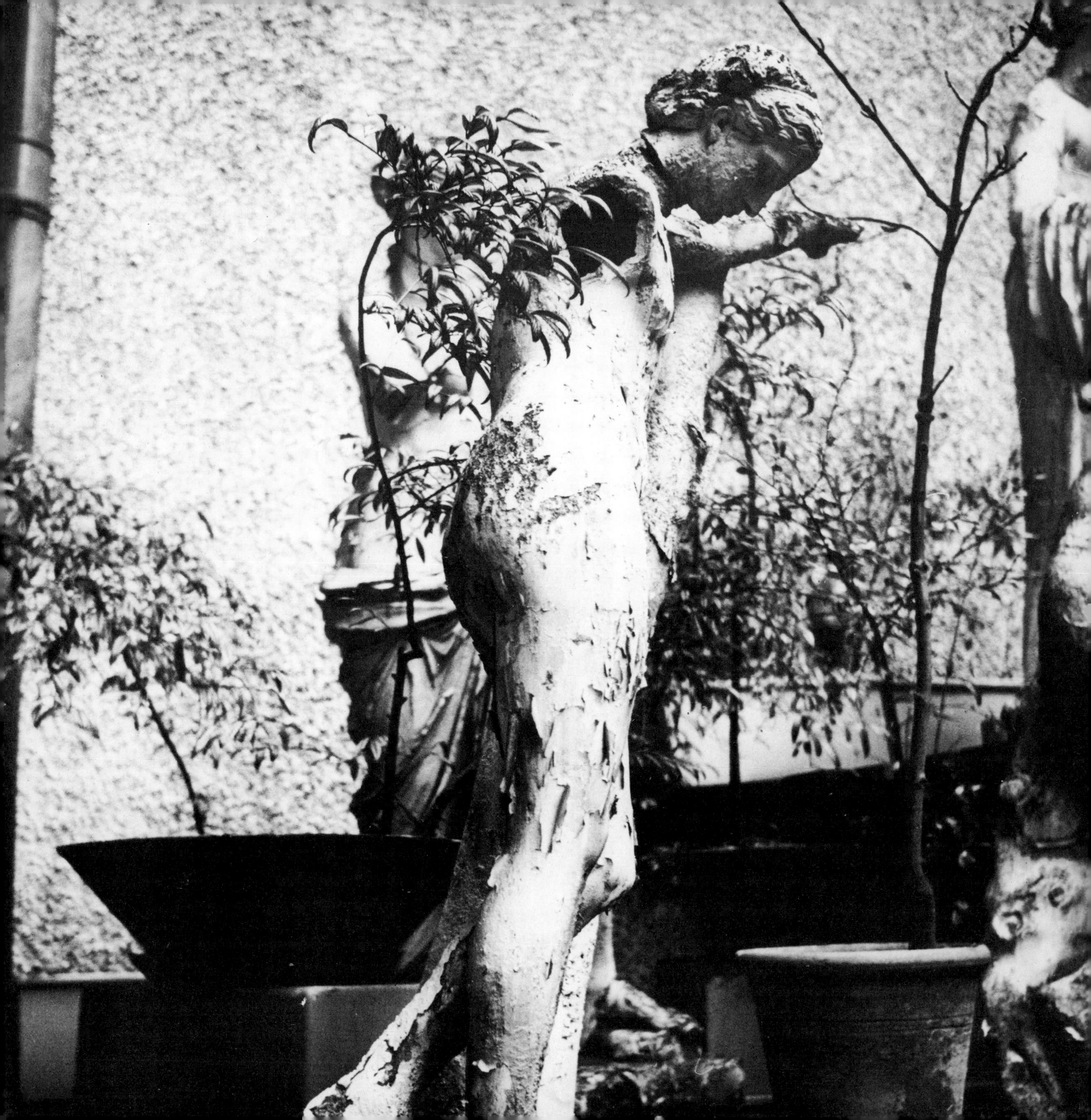

kept the house under control, to such a degree that even intimates of the family never felt that they could bring just any casual, occasional, one-night partner to the Joyce's apartment, it had to be a relationship of a more permanent nature.

She watched over his health, with good reason. He suffered acutely from iritis, a painful and distressing inflammation of the eye. Several operations did not cure the problem. Drinking inflamed the condition: Nora consequently behaved with considerable aggression towards tempters.

It was an ordinary house, the Blooms', convenient to shops, churches, schools and public transport. The occupants had some pretensions, sufficient prudence. Molly is thirty-four, the daughter of a soldier, a disappointed wife. Is Molly Bloom's soliloquy no more than Joyce's idea of how a woman's mind works? Or, to be more accurate, how he would like to *believe* a woman's mind works? Lying in the dark she ranges over the full scope of her sexual imagination, recalling her lurid afternoon activities with Boylan. Every man she has known is mentioned either directly or obliquely: her husband's sexual predilections draw comment: ". . . drawers drawers the whole blessed time till I promised to give him the pair off my doll to carry about in his waistcoat pocket . . ."

Once, in Dublin, Joyce and Gogarty played a practical joke on the celibate National Librarian. They stretched a pair of drawers across a chair, strategically accosted them with a propped-up broom handle, placarded it "John Eglinton". Friends at a restaurant table recall Joyce taking out a tiny pair of drawers and fingerwalking it across the table. Jung reading *Ulysses,* told Joyce that "the forty pages of non stop run in the end is a string of veritable psychological peaches". Joyce referred to Jung as "the Swiss Tweedledum, not to

be confused with the Austrian Tweedledee, Freud".

Joyce's Ulysses has won too. He has returned to his palace, defeated his suitors. Molly may have been unfaithful, but she lies in his bed beside him now, albeit upside down: peace, reason and consideration have carried the day.

When Joyce was buried in the cemetery at Zurich in the Friedhofkpalle, it was cold and snowing. Only a few people stood there. The cemetery adjoins the zoological gardens, which pleased Nora. She said he was "awfully fond of the lions" and it pleased her to imagine him lying there and hearing them roar. She lived on in Zurich, lonely, unheeding of what went on in the world of literature which had beaten a path to her husband's door. She paid no attention to any other writers: when you have been married "to the greatest writer in the world, how could you be thinking of the little ones". She died in 1951 and the priest who spoke at her funeral described her as "a great sinner".

Molly hears the clock chime. She thinks of the day they spent out in Howth gazing down on the island of Ireland's Eye, she thinks of the time Poldy called her a flower of the mountain, ". . . and first I put my arms around him yes and drew him down to me so he could feel my breasts all perfume yes and his heart was going like mad and yes I said yes I will Yes". The clock has struck at a quarter past two in the morning at the end of Bloomsday.

A friend was arranging a birthday party for Joyce and even though he was depressed he didn't object. "Birth, departure, sickness, death, life is so tragic we are permitted to distract ourselves and forget a little . . ."

Exiled in Trieste, in Zurich, in Paris, whenever, James Joyce closed his eyes every day and took a walk around Dublin . . .

POSTSCRIPT

He wore a white coat, dentist-like: it enhanced the light by which to write. Those who met him commented on the high forehead and how disconcerting the thickness of the spectacles was. He wrote to his daughter when her mind was troubled to the point of illness: "Why do you always sit at the window? No doubt it makes a pretty picture but a girl walking in the fields also makes a pretty picture."

Facts, facts, facts: as he immured himself within them, behind them, so they pursue him, in town and gown. At dinner in Dublin people argue over his frailties as though he had just left the room. In academe his epiphanies provide agonised, ambitious conversation. A mark of distinction, like a physical characteristic, is claimed by those whose relatives or ancestors were mentioned in his books.

Now that the embarrassment surrounding him is dying – it was the result of a conflict between distaste and liberalism – Ireland will take pride in James Joyce who wrote, they say, "the most difficult of entertaining novels and the most entertaining of difficult ones". Remember that he was spreadeagled by abusers. He loved to quote, in a paranoid wallow, the tale of the man who asked for *Ulysses* in a Dublin bookshop. The bookseller did not stock it, much to the customer's delight. "The man who wrote it," he trumpeted, "had better not come back to Ireland – ever." Hot on the heels of this delicious terror came Joyce's defence to a relative: "If *Ulysses* isn't fit to read, life isn't fit to live –" pause – "of *course* life is fit to live – and *Ulysses* to read."

When it emerged from the embroidery of proofs – he corrected up to six sets of galleys – *Ulysses* stimulated, broadly, three responses. First came an undoubted, if intellectually fashionable, appreciation – albeit from those who had been pre-conditioned by the *Little Review* serialisation, or by respectful word-of-mouth, or by regard for the author's earlier works. Elsewhere, distaste, running up the scale to disgust. To this opinion clung several critics (including Virginia Woolf and Alfred Noyes), the American legal system, the British customs authorities and the Irish nation who, presciently, did not need to read *Ulysses* in order to establish the fact that it ought to be burned. A third school was bewildered – by the language, by the exhilarated tapestries woven by the author, by his mixture of erudition and cunning; readers either fell away completely, or came eventually to enjoy, to be consumed.

The publication was, still is, one of the great dates in literary history. When the first two copies arrived in Paris Joyce was happily talismanned. It was his fortieth birthday: the first two copies of the thousand in the limited edition were numbers 901 and 902, and the next two he received from the printer's steaming, erratic press were 251 and 252: buyers kept calling at Sylvia Beach's shop on the day – the word had wildfired – only to be disappointed for lack of copies: the copy numbered "1" was presented by post – he did much of his own packaging and dispatching – to his great patron, Harriet Shaw Weaver (whose very surname he found engagingly satisfying) and the first review, a month after publication, in the London *Observer* brought requests by the next post for 136 copies. A second edition, published eight months later, in

October 1922, at two guineas per copy, sold its entire two thousand copies in four days.

A new planet had, therefore, appeared in Joyce's skies. His letters to his friends were dominated by the orbit of *Ulysses*: the comments of the critics, the attitudes of the public, the reactions of the booksellers, were rehearsed again and again. To one friend he advised that he ought not "throw *Ulysses* out of the window. Pyrrhus was killed in Argos like that. Also Socrates might be passing in the street." To a relative who had given or lent her copy – which though unsigned was immediately worth forty pounds in London: "There is a difference between a present of a pound of chops and a present of a book like *Ulysses*. You can acknowledge receipt of a present of a pound of chops by simply nodding gratefully, supposing, that is, you have your mouth full of as much of the chops as it will conveniently hold, but you cannot do so with a large book on account of the difficulty of fitting it into the mouth."

For whatever reasons, and despite the book's alleged obscurity, *Ulysses* and Joyce eventually became fixed in the popular mind – even in Ireland. Whether for notoriety, or for the fact that he was iconoclastic, he clamped a hold, even on the minds of those who were never expected to read him. I have heard bank clerks revelling in his language: Molly Bloom was taken, unwittingly, to Confession; an artist in Dublin, Jewish, sensitive and shrewd, dresses now as Leopold Bloom, walks the city bowler-hatted and wistful.

Joyce once wrote to Nora: "Dublin is a detestable city and the people in it are most repulsive to me", but he was nonetheless quintessentially Irish. There is a myth, accepted by the world, not denied by the natives, that the Irish are a warm, friendly people. Not wholly true: that open, hospitable spirit is as the rind on cheese. Caution is the decree of experience – historically, friendship and easy confidence often led to betrayal, to the militia, to the landlord. Abroad, James Joyce was able to build upon this aloofness, a stranger among strangers. He may have been surrounded by friends, acquaintances, fellow-writers (many of whom made a reputation by having known Joyce while they and he were in the same place at the same time), he may have entertained at his favourite restaurants when he was in funds and in Paris – but he chose distance.

There are other manifestations of Joyce's Irishry – contradictions in speech, in language, as with the small boy's jibe: "Eh, mister, your fly is open, mister," whereas in English such form of address indicates politeness. There is the need too – chronically Hibernian – to identify with somebody of historical or spiritual significance. When the poet Yeats made a rich and honeyed filibuster in the Irish Senate, a scarcely-lettered colleague, who had difficulty with articulation and pronunciation, sprang to his feet and cawed: "Jaysus, Mr. Yates – you took the very words outa me mouth." And Joyce, delighted, discovered that he had a physical parallel too with his Classical mentor, blind Homer, "blind from glaucoma according to one of my doctors, Dr. Berman, as iridectomy [Joyce's own complaint] had not been thought of."

Joyce signifies frustration. The endlessness of his enlightenment breeds feeble mortality. One scholar of my acquaintance claims that he can point out over seven hundred liminal and subliminal references, connections, jokes, puns, on the first page of *Finnegans Wake*. Joyce tantalises too: there is trickery in every paragraph, every sentence, a new meaning with each sighting. Further frustration then – the desire of the writer to keep secrets seems to transfer itself to the reader: does one shout the discovery or not? (Which may be the reason why "Penelope" is the shortest chapter in this book.) Does it explain too, why Joyce as an author and a subject of study arouses such feelings of possessiveness? The interest which students of Joyce exhibit in each other's work-in-progress amounts to a form of industrial espionage and every new thesis, unless its scholarship is incontrovertible (well-nigh impossible, even for an Ellmann, a Burgess, a Groden or a Gilbert) is challenged to a frazzle.

What, finally (taking one's words in one's hands), attracts so many people to this pied piper? That his claim is true, that he has contained the universal in his particular? Or humanity? Real and imagined, it belied his acerbity. Once, Nora threatened to leave him and commenced an explanatory letter to her mother with a small "i". Joyce wondered humorously over her shoulder whether such an event did not merit at least a capital letter. "Counterparts", a story in *Dubliners*, ends: "The boy uttered a squeal of pain as the stick cut his thigh. He clasped his hands together in the air and his voice shook with fright. 'Oh, pa!' he cried. 'Don't beat me, pa! And I'll . . . I'll say a Hail Mary for you . . . I'll say a Hail Mary for you, pa, if you don't beat me . . . I'll say a Hail Mary . . .'" To his daughter, Lucia, Joyce wrote: "The trees you love change their leaves with the passing of the months" and promised to send her cuttings from newspaper articles about him or the family where her name was mentioned. Mr. Bloom bought buns for the seagulls because he first fooled them with a throwaway piece of paper.

Where *Ulysses* is concerned his appeal must also be the way in which he omnipotently contained Dublin and its inhabitants. One visiting Joycean student expressed the wish that all the Dublin of *Ulysses* would collapse and disappear (the City Fathers and town planners are doing their damnable best) in order to have the sheer comfort of imagination only. And the marvel of the Joycean achievement often becomes too much to encompass – *Ulysses* was created before he was forty years old.

And is it in that dimension, in his web of Dublin, that all the strands of James Joyce are drawn together? Human beings and their habitations are the subject of literature, since we have little else to write about. Joyce drew together the city and the world and all the inhabitants therein residing – a dolls' house, a shelf of specimens.

With customary monumental arrogance he had stated early in life that he wished to "forge the uncreated conscience" of his race, that he would do so grandiosely by going forth to greet experience. Contradictorily, he chose a simple vehicle for his journey forth, the day on which he came to love. Some lovers have written symphonies, some have built temples. Infinitely and multitudinously, James Joyce wrote *Ulysses*.

Entrance
to The National Library and
The National College of Art

BIBLIOGRAPHY

A note on the bibliography: The books listed here are those which have proved particularly useful in the preparation of *James Joyce's Odyssey*. If a full bibliography were to be included there would neither be space enough nor time enough: many references come from memory and have been gathered through the years from books on Joyce, Dublin and Ireland.

Allen, Walter, *The Short Story in English,* Clarendon Press, Oxford, England, 1981.

Anderson, Chester G., *James Joyce and His World,* Thames and Hudson, London, 1967.

Blamires, Harry, *The Bloomsday Book,* Methuen and Co., London, 1966.

Budgen, Frank, *James Joyce and the Making of Ulysses,* Indiana University Press, Bloomington, 1960.

Burgess, Anthony, *Joysprick – An Introduction to the Language of James Joyce,* André Deutsch, London, 1973.

Craig, Maurice, *Dublin, 1660-1860,* 1952.

Ellman, Richard, *James Joyce,* Oxford University Press, 1959.
(Ed.) *Letters of James Joyce*, Vols. II and III, Faber and Faber, 1966.
James Joyce's Tower, Eastern Regional Tourism Organisation, Dun Laoire, Dublin, 1969.
Ulysses on the Liffey, Faber and Faber, London, 1972.
Yeats – The Man and the Masks, Macmillan, London, 1949.

Gilbert, Stuart, *James Joyce's "Ulysses" – A Study:* New York, 1930.
(Ed.) *Letters of James Joyce,* Vol. I: Faber and Faber, London, 1957.

Groden, Michael, *Ulysses in Progress,* Princeton University Press, 1977.

Hart, Clive and Knuth, Leo, *A Topographical Guide to James Joyce's "Ulysses":* Pub. by "A Wake Newslitter", Department of Literature, Essex University, England, 1975.

Hickey, D. J. and J. E., *A Dictionary of Irish History since 1800,* Gill and Macmillan, Dublin, 1980.

Hutchins, Patricia, *James Joyce's Dublin,* London, 1950.

Jeffares, A. Norman, *W. B. Yeats, Man and Poet,* Routledge and Kegan Paul, London, 1949.

Joyce, James, *Ulysses,* first published, Shakespeare and Co., Paris, 1922; Bodley Head, London, 1936; Penguin Books, Harmondsworth, Middlesex, England 1969. In the U.S. first published, Random House, 1934.
Dubliners, Grant Richards, London, 1914; B.W. Huebsch

(later of Viking Press), New York, 1916; Jonathan Cape, London, 1967; Granada Publishing, London (in Panther Books), 1977.
A Portrait of the Artist as a Young Man, B.W. Huebsch (later of Viking Press), New York, 1916; Jonathan Cape, London, 1924; Penguin Books, 1960.
Finnegans Wake, Faber and Faber, London, 1939; Viking Press, New York, 1939.

Kenner, Hugh, *Joyce's Voices,* Faber and Faber, London, 1978.

Lyon, F. S. L., *James Joyce's Dublin,* Twentieth-Century Studies, IV, November 1970.

Lyons, J. B., *Oliver St. John Gogarty* – a Biography, Blackwater Press, Dublin, 1980.

McHugh, Roland, *Annotations to "Finnegans Wake",* Routledge and Kegan Paul, London, 1980.

McLoughlin, Adrian, *Guide to Historic Dublin,* Gill and Macmillan, Dublin, 1979.

O'Connor, Ulick, *Oliver St. John Gogarty,* Jonathan Cape, London, 1964, Granada Publishing, London, 1981.

Peake, C. H., *James Joyce – the Citizen and the Artist,* Edward Arnold, London, 1977

Power, Arthur, *Conversations with James Joyce,* Millington Books, London, 1974.

Raleigh, John Henry, *The Chronicle of Leopold and Molly Bloom,* University of California Press, Berkeley, 1977.

Ryan, John, (Ed.) *A Bash in the Tunnel: James Joyce by the Irish*, Clifton Books, London, 1970.
Remembering How We Stood, Gill and Macmillan, Dublin, 1975.

Schleifer, Ronald, *The Genres of the Irish Literary Revival,* Pilgrim Books, Norman, Oklahoma and Wolfhound Press, Dublin, 1980.

Shewring, Walter, (Trans) *The Odyssey* by Homer, Oxford University Press, England, 1980.

Somerville-Large, Peter, *Dublin,* Hamish Hamilton, London, 1979.

Thom's Official Directory of the United Kingdom of Great Britain and Ireland, 1904, London, 1905.

ACKNOWLEDGMENTS

The author wishes to make acknowledgment, with gratitude, to the following:

The Bodley Head in London, and Random House, Inc. in New York for permission to quote extensively from *Ulysses*; Faber & Faber in London and Viking Press in New York for permission to quote from *My Brother's Keeper* by Stanislaus Joyce; from *The Letters of James Joyce* edited by Stuart Gilbert (Vol. I) and Richard Ellmann, (Vols. II & III); Jonathan Cape in London and Viking Press in New York for permission to quote from *A Portrait of the Artist as a Young Man* and *Dubliners*; to the Society of Authors protecting the Literary Estate of James Joyce for permission to quote from *The Holy Office*; Faber & Faber in London for permission to quote from *Dublin* by Louis MacNeice; Sir Osbert Lancaster and John Murray Ltd. for permission to quote from *Afternoons with Baedeker* in *Facades and Faces*; to the Representatives of the late Seumas O'Sullivan for permission to quote from his works; Mr. Oliver D. Gogarty for permission to quote from the works of the late Dr. Oliver St. John Gogarty; Mr. Michael Yeats for permission to quote from *Who Goes with Fergus* by the late W. B. Yeats; The Ordnance Survey of Ireland, Phoenix Park, Dublin for permission to reproduce and quote from maps of Dublin – Permit No. 3631; Dr. Alf MacLochlainn, Director of the National Library of Ireland, Kildare Street, Dublin, for permission to reproduce pictures from the Lawrence Collection and his Staff for their unflagging courtesy and assistance; to the Trustees of the British Museum in London for permission to reproduce the Plan of Dublin as of 1904, and to the staff of the Map Room in the British Museum for such diligent effort on the author's behalf; to Mr. Patrick Long, Director of the Eastern Regional Tourism Board, Dun Laoghaire, Co. Dublin and to Mr. Robert Nicholson, Curator of the James Joyce Museum in Sandycove for their kind permission to quote from the ticket of admission to the Museum and to photograph the Museum and its exhibits; to the Master and Staff of the National Maternity Hospital in Dublin for permission to photograph within the hospital; to the Directors of Arthur Guinness, Son & Company Ltd. for permission to photograph from their rooftops; to Mike O'Malley and Ray Hollidge of Chartwell Illustrations, Ltd., Croydon, Surrey, for the chapter maps.

Gratitude born of admiration is due to Professor Richard Ellman; it is impossible to progress with any research into the world of James Joyce without relying heavily on Professor Ellmann's unrivalled scholarship in the field; likewise Dr. Anthony Burgess, who supplied words of kind encouragement; Roland McHugh's example and enthusiasm are daunting and exhilarating, Vivien Igoe uncovered some extra and enthralling sources and Ulick O'Connor offered assistance unselfishly.

Acknowledgments of a particular kind are due to Sharyn Troughton of Hodder & Stoughton who designed this book with affection and zeal; to Ion Trewin who as Senior Non-Fiction Editor edited it and nursed it into life; to Clare Bristow who transfused it, Amanda Batten who guarded it, Tracy Loveman who typed it impeccably; to Jorge Lewinski for taking an interpretative as well as a photographic role – and to Brigid Roden who helped so competently in all sorts of ways.

INDEX

PLAN OF

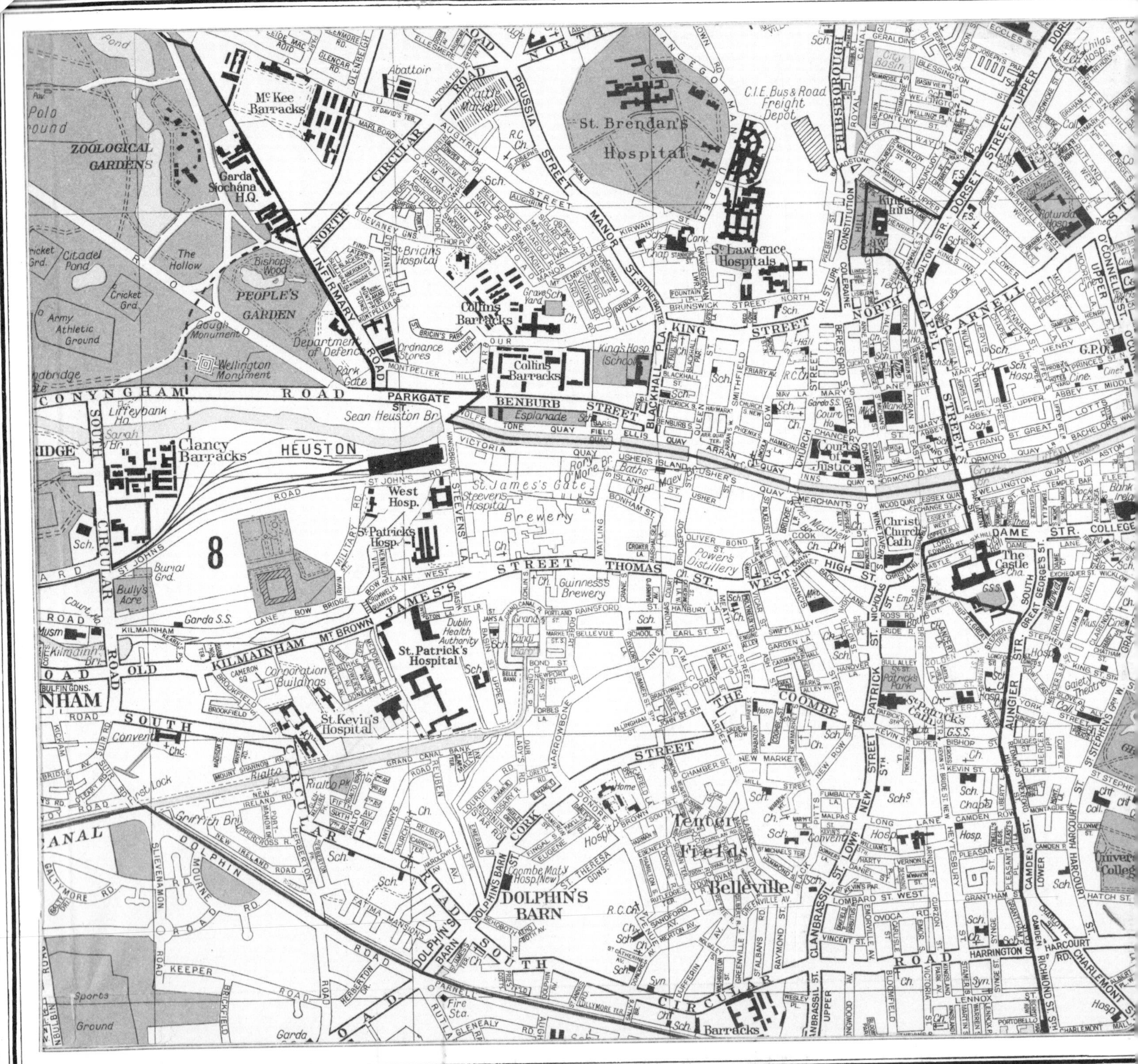

ZOOLOGICAL GARDENS
Polo Ground
Pond
Mc Kee Barracks
Garda Síochána H.Q.
Abattoir
Cattle Market
St. Brendan's Hospital
C.I.E. Bus & Road Freight Depot
City Basin
Cricket Grd.
Citadel Pond
The Hollow
Bishops Wood
PEOPLE'S GARDEN
Army Athletic Ground
Gough Monument
Wellington Monument
Department of Defence
Park Gate
Ordnance Stores
St. Bricin's Hospital
Collins Barracks
King's Hosp. (School)
St. Lawrence Hospitals
King's Inns
Rotunda Hosp.
Courts of Justice
G.P.O.
CONYNGHAM ROAD
PARKGATE ST.
BENBURB STREET
Sean Heuston Br.
Liffeybank Ho.
Sarah Br.
Clancy Barracks
HEUSTON
Esplanade
WOLFE TONE QUAY
ELLIS QUAY
ARRAN QUAY
INNS QUAY
ORMOND QUAY
WELLINGTON QUAY
Rory O'More Br.
Queen Maev Br.
St. James's Gate Brewery
Steevens Hospital
West Hosp.
St. Patrick's Hosp.
8
Burial Grd.
Bully's Acre
Court Ho.
Musm.
Kilmainham Br.
Garda S.S.
ST. JOHN'S ROAD
SOUTH CIRCULAR ROAD
JAMES'S STREET
THOMAS ST.
Guinness's Brewery
Power's Distillery
Dublin Health Authority
St. Patrick's Hospital
Grand Canal Harb.
KILMAINHAM
OLD KILMAINHAM
Corporation Buildings
St. Kevin's Hospital
Convent
Rialto Br.
Rialto Pk.
First Lock
Griffith Br.
GRAND CANAL
Christ Church Cath.
The Castle
DAME STR.
COLLEGE
HIGH ST.
THE COOMBE
St. Patrick's Park
St. Patrick's Cath.
Gaiety Theatre
Tenter Fields
Belleville
Coombe Maty. Hosp. (New)
DOLPHIN'S BARN
DOLPHIN ROAD
Fatima Mansions
CLANBRASSIL ST.
NEW STREET STH.
AUNGIER STR.
CAMDEN ST.
HARCOURT ST.
CHARLEMONT ST.
University College
Barracks
Fire Sta.
Sports Ground
CIRCULAR ROAD